REBIRTH THROUGH ALIGNMENT
By:
Kiarra Schmidt

Rebirth Through Alignment

© 2025 Kiarra Schmidt

All rights reserved.

Printed in the United States of America

First Edition

ISBN: 9798279031481

This is a work of memoir. Names, details, and identifying characteristics may have been changed to protect privacy.

Dedication

For the version of me who kept going without knowing where she was headed.
For the moments I felt lost, heavy, and unsure; and stayed anyway.
For the nights I asked for clarity in silence, not realizing I was already changing.

For everyone who has felt the quiet ache of becoming.
For those who carried what was never theirs.
For those who learned the hard way that growth is not loud; it's honest.

This book is for anyone who chose to listen inward when the world was noisy.
Those who trusted themselves before they had proof.
Those who didn't break — they shined.

Author's Note

This book was not written all at once. It came together slowly, in pieces — through reflection, silence, and the moments that linger after life changes shape. What you are holding is not a guide or a set of instructions, but a record of becoming.

Some experiences are difficult to name while you are living them. Writing this book was part of learning to sit with them honestly, without needing to explain or resolve everything.

Read this in your own time. Take what resonates. Leave what doesn't. And trust that whatever led you here is part of your own unfolding.

Rebirth Through Alignment

By: Kiarra Schmidt

CHAPTER 1 — A Life Moving Fast

Before the crash, before the stillness, before everything in me shifted, life felt like a road that stretched endlessly in front of me — fast, loud, and demanding. I didn't realize how quickly I was moving or how easily I slipped into the rhythm of surviving. Every day I woke up and stepped into a world that expected something from me, even when I didn't know what I expected from myself.

There were mornings I would look in the mirror and see a version of myself that was doing her best but wasn't fully living. I wasn't unhappy — that's the strange thing. I wasn't lost, but I wasn't anchored either. I was floating through my days, checking boxes, showing up, doing everything I thought a strong person should do. But underneath all that, there was a quiet ache I couldn't name. It wasn't sadness. It was something more subtle: an inner knowing that this wasn't my final form.

Life felt heavy and light at the same time. Heavy with responsibility, memories, expectations — light with moments of laughter, small joys, the warmth of people I loved. I thought that was balanced. I thought that was how life was supposed to be. Some days you feel everything, some days you feel nothing, and you just keep going.

But even then, something inside me was shifting. I just didn't know it yet.

There were signs — small ones — that I ignored without meaning too. Times when my body felt tired in a way sleep couldn't fix. Times when my mind felt loud even in silence. Times when my heart felt full and empty in the same breath. I thought I was just overthinking. I thought I was just being "too much." But now I understand those were moments where God was trying to get my attention, not to scare me, but to prepare me.

Life was teaching me before I even knew I was learning.

I didn't know then that I was carrying things that weren't mine. Other people's fears. Other people's disappointments. Their doubts. Their assumptions about who I should be, how I should act, what I should prioritize. I took all of it and tucked it neatly into my chest as if it belonged to me. I didn't even realize how heavy it was until it was gone.

There were days I felt like I understood people too deeply. I could see their intentions, their patterns, their pain — and I took it on without knowing how to set it down. I thought that meant I was strong. I thought that meant I was mature. Looking back, it meant I hadn't learned yet that empathy without boundaries becomes exhaustion. It weighs. It becomes a quiet drowning.

Still, I kept going. That was something I was proud of: I always kept going.

At the time, I didn't know where I was heading. I didn't have a perfect plan for my life. I was figuring it out like everyone else. But I always moved with a sense of purpose, even if I couldn't explain it to anyone. There was always something in me that knew I was meant for more — not in a flashy, dramatic way, but in a quiet internal pull. A feeling that there was a version of me waiting to be revealed. A version who wasn't weighed down. A version who wasn't confused. A version who wasn't afraid.

But before shift comes pressure. Before clarity comes chaos. Before new life comes a breaking point.

The days leading up to the crash were strangely normal. I woke up, went through my routines, thought the same thoughts, worried about the same small things. I was living, but I wasn't fully aware of myself. And that is the most dangerous kind of living — where you move automatically, without noticing your spirit slipping further and further into autopilot.

I didn't see it coming. I couldn't have. But life was building toward a moment that would change everything — not to punish me, but to realign me. My soul already knew. My body already felt it. I just hadn't caught up yet.

Looking back, the signs were everywhere:
The feeling that something had to change
The heaviness I couldn't explain
The moments of clarity that came out of nowhere
The quiet restlessness in my chest
The internal whisper: You're becoming someone new.

I pushed through it all, thinking that was just life. That everyone felt this way. But now I understand that when something in your life is about to shift, you feel it. Even before you know why.

I was moving quickly but learning slowly. I was growing but didn't know it. I was shedding layers I hadn't realized were no longer mine. And all of that — the pace, the pressure, the quiet transformation — was leading me to a moment that would stop everything and restart everything at the same time.

I didn't know it yet, but my life was about to split into two parts:

Before the crash.
And after it.

Everything I was carrying would be stripped away. Everything unclear would sharpen into focus. Everything I thought mattered would fade, and everything I had overlooked would rise to the center.

This chapter of my life wasn't about darkness. It wasn't about tragedy. It was about preparation — God preparing me for the person I would soon become.

And even though I didn't know it then, I was already walking toward the moment that would save me, break me open, and rebuild me all in one breath.

This was the life I lived before I opened my eyes in the wreckage.
This was who I was before I became who I am.

CHAPTER 2 — Moments That Shape Us

Long before the crash, before the prayer, before the turning point that would realign my entire spirit, my life was already being stitched together by small moments that didn't seem important at the time. It's funny how the things we overlook end up becoming the foundation of everything we become. The big events get all the attention, but it's the quiet, everyday moments that shape us the most — the things we feel, the decisions we make, the lessons we repeat until we finally understand them.

When I look back now, I can see the patterns clearly. I can see how each season of my life was preparing me for the moment everything stopped. I can see how each person, each hurt, each joy, each mistake, and each blessing played a part in shaping my heart. I wasn't just living; I was building the person I would need to be in order to survive what was coming — and to rise after it.

I grew up learning how to read people without meaning to. I paid attention to energy, tone, and unspoken emotions. I could feel when someone was hurting even when they pretended they weren't. I could sense tension before it became words. I understood motives when people didn't want to admit them out loud. At the time, I thought that was normal. I thought everyone carried that level of awareness.

What I didn't realize was that this sensitivity wasn't just a trait — it was a gift. A heavy one at times, yes, but still a gift. And it prepared me for the life I would eventually live: a life built on understanding, on compassion, on guidance, on seeing past the surface.

But gifts can feel like burdens when you don't know how to handle them.

I often took on more than I needed to. Other people's pain became mine. Other people's stress stuck to me like dust. I would absorb emotions that weren't even meant for me. I didn't know how to separate what I felt from what wasn't mine. I carried it all without being asked.

And yet, that same ability to feel deeply is what taught me to survive. It's what taught me to connect. It's what taught me to lead with my heart even when the world around me didn't understand why I cared so much.

There were moments in my childhood and teenage years that I didn't know were shaping me:
Conversations I overheard
Feelings I learned to swallow
Trust I gave too easily
Times I had to be stronger than I wanted to be
Silent prayers I whispered without knowing who I was talking to
Nights when my thoughts kept me awake because they felt too big for my age

All of that — every piece — was molding me.

There were also moments of joy, moments that lit something inside me. Laughter with people I loved. Adventures that made me feel free. Times when I felt seen, understood, and valued. Those were the moments that fed my spirit, even when I didn't realize how hungry I was. They became the memories I would carry into every dark moment of my future, the ones that reminded me I was more than my struggles.

But most of all, I was shaped by the times life didn't make sense.

The times I asked Why?
Why me?

Why this?
Why now?

The times when pain hits harder than it should have.
The times when change came too quickly.
The times when people left without explanation.
The times when I carried wounds that weren't visible to the world.

Life teaches us through contrast.

We learn what we want by experiencing what we don't want.
We learn who we are by learning who we're not.
We learn strength by being placed in situations where we have none left.

And I went through all of that before the crash — without realizing I was being prepared.

That preparation didn't feel like preparation. It felt like life was happening to me. It felt like growing up. It felt like trying, failing, loving, hurting, healing a little, hurting again, and still waking up each day trying to figure everything out.

But now I understand something I couldn't see then:

All those moments were making my heart resilient.
They were carving into me the depth I would need to rebuild myself.
They were strengthening the voice inside me that would one day guide others.
They were aligning me with purpose long before I knew I even had one.

There is a reason God builds you quietly before He shifts you loudly.
There is a reason your spirit feels too big before your life makes space for it.

There is a reason you go through seasons where nothing feels stable — because you are being stretched, molded, sharpened.

Every moment before the crash was part of a story I didn't understand yet. I wasn't meant to understand it then. I was only meant to live it, to feel it, to carry it, to grow through it. It's only now, looking back with new eyes, that I can see how carefully God arranged every detail.

The crash didn't start my transformation — it revealed it. Everything I had lived before that moment was building the person who would walk out of that wreckage alive, awake, and spiritually reborn.

This chapter of my life wasn't about pain; it was about foundation.
It wasn't about suffering; it was about strengthening.
It wasn't about confusion; it was about preparation.

I didn't know it then, but each moment was shaping me into someone who would one day say:

I survived for a reason.
I was saved for a purpose.
And I will live every day honoring the second life I was given.

This was the quiet shaping.
The unseen molding.
The preparation for everything that came after.

CHAPTER 3 — The Prayer That Opened the Door

There are moments in life that don't seem significant until you look back and realize they were the doorway to everything that followed. Not the crash, not the impact — but the prayer the night before. A prayer whispered with no expectation, no warning, no idea that it would echo into the next day and split my entire life in half.

I didn't know I was preparing myself.
I didn't know God was listening so closely.
I didn't know I was about to be answered in a way that would change my entire existence.

All I knew was that something in me felt heavy, and I needed to let it out.

It wasn't a dramatic moment. There were no tears, no breakdown, no music in the background, nothing that looked like a life-changing scene from a movie. It was just me — quiet, tired, thoughtful — feeling a weight in my chest I couldn't name. A weight I had been carrying for months without realizing how deeply it sat inside me.

And for the first time in a long time...
I stopped running from it.
I stopped distracting myself.
I stopped pretending everything was fine.

Instead, I opened my heart in the simplest, rawest way.

I didn't pray for safety.
I didn't pray for protection.
I didn't pray for blessings or success or answers.

I prayed for alignment.

I prayed for the version of myself I felt deep inside — the version I had brushed aside, the version I didn't feel ready to become. I asked for clarity. I asked for strength. I asked for whatever was blocking me to finally break. I asked God to help me shed everything that wasn't meant for me so I could finally step into who I truly was.

I didn't know what I was asking for.
Not fully.
Not consciously.
But my spirit knew.

Sometimes our soul prays before our mind understands why.

That night, I asked to become who I was meant to be. I asked to feel free. I asked to be shown my truth in the clearest way possible. I asked for a shift — not knowing shifts rarely come gently.

What I didn't understand then is that God doesn't answer prayers halfway.
When you ask for alignment, He removes everything that isn't aligned.
When you ask for the truth, He exposes what you've been avoiding.
When you ask for clarity, He shakes you awake.
When you ask to find yourself, He takes you through the places you lost yourself.

I didn't realize I had prayed for transformation — real transformation — the kind that doesn't just change your habits but rewires your spirit.

It was a simple prayer, quiet and unplanned, but it opened a spiritual doorway. It was the beginning of the unraveling, the beginning of the stripping away, the beginning of my rebirth.

And the next day, life answered.

Not cruelly.
Not violently.
Not as punishment.
But as an awakening.

I didn't feel fear after that prayer — I felt something else. A strange calm. Strange knowing. Like something inside me had already decided what needed to happen. Like my soul was stepping forward while my mind was still trying to catch up.

There are moments in life where God prepares you in silence before He moves you in magnitude.
This was that moment.

The prayer didn't feel powerful at the time. It felt like a release.
Like surrender.
Like finally letting go of the fight I had with myself.

I didn't ask God to change my life.
I asked Him to change me.

And he did — in the most unexpected way.

The next day, I would find myself in a situation that would force me to face everything I had asked for: truth, alignment, purpose, clarity, surrender.

This prayer wasn't a coincidence.
It wasn't random.
It was the doorway.

The crash wasn't the start.
The prayer was.

It was the moment I unknowingly opened the door to the next version of my life — the version that would walk away from the wreckage not broken, but awakened. Not lost, but aligned. Not afraid, but deeply, undeniably alive.

I had asked for transformation.
And transformation was already on its way.

CHAPTER 4 — The Impact

The morning of the crash didn't feel different. That's the part that still lingers in my memory—how ordinary everything seemed, how normal the air felt, how unaware I was that life was quietly rearranging itself behind the scenes. There were no warnings, no signs, no strange feelings that something was coming. I woke up and stepped into the day the way I always did, carrying the same thoughts, the same concerns, the same quiet restlessness that had lived in my chest for months.

Looking back, it amazes me how a life can change on a day that starts out so unremarkably silent.

I moved through my routine with the same distracted energy I always carried, not knowing that the prayer I whispered the night before had already begun reshaping my path. I felt a stillness inside me that morning—a calmness I didn't yet understand. Not peace exactly, but a slowing down of something internal, like my spirit had stepped forward while the rest of me lagged behind.

I didn't know it yet, but I was walking into the moment that would divide my life into a "before" and an "after."

When I got into the car, my mind was racing the way it often did, but my heart felt strangely quiet. My hands found the wheel out of habit. The world outside the windshield looked the same, but something in the air felt paused, suspended, like time was holding its breath.

And then everything changed.

It happened faster than thought—faster than fear, faster than any human instinct. One moment I was in control, and the next the world around me exploded into motion. Metal twisted. Light fractured. The sound was both deafening and distant, as if it was happening underwater. The car spun, and yet, inside me, something slowed down.

I felt like a deer in the headlights. I knew no matter how much control I had, someone would still slip through and change my life. For better, for worse.

There was a pocket of silence in the middle of the chaos. A moment where everything inside me became still, even though everything outside me was falling apart. Time didn't stretch; it deepened. It pulled me into a space where fear had no meaning.

In that suspended breath, I felt acceptance.

I felt clarity.

I felt myself understanding something I had never understood before: death does not always come with terror. Sometimes it comes with truth.

I remember thinking, This might be it.
And instead of panic, I felt peace.

A strange, overwhelming peace that didn't belong to this world.

My original thought wasn't regret. It wasn't fear of losing my life. It wasn't sadness for what I hadn't done. The only thing that rose from me was a prayer, pure and instinctive, as if it had been waiting for this exact moment.

"Lord… please help and guide everyone I have ever encountered and even glanced at. Let my family and loved ones know that I love them. Let them know I lived for myself and I am proud of who I was becoming. And let no one lose their way because of me."

It was the purest form of surrender I had ever experienced. Not surrender to death—but surrender to truth. To love. To Purpose.

Nothing else mattered in that moment. Not the past, not the future, not my mistakes, not the things I wished I had done differently. What mattered was connection. What mattered was love. What mattered was knowing that my life—however long or short—had meaning.

The world outside continued to crash and spin, but inside me something opened. Something released. Something aligned. I wasn't afraid. I wasn't fighting. I wasn't holding on to anything I couldn't take with me.

And then, just as suddenly as it began, everything stopped.

The noise faded.
The motion slowed.
Reality softened back into shape.

And then…I opened my eyes.

Alive.

Breathing.

Here.

But not the same.

The world looked different, not because anything around me had changed, but because something inside me had. The air felt sharper. My thoughts felt quieter. My heart felt weightless and heavy all at once. I didn't know how to explain it; I just knew I had crossed a line I wasn't meant to stay on the other side of.

To know that I was still alive, still walking, still capable of moving through this world—that alone felt like a blessing that could never be measured.

The impact didn't just break the car.

It broke the version of me that was never meant to survive.

It cracked open everything unnecessary.
It stripped away everything false.
It forced me into alignment with the prayer I had whispered the night before.

I didn't walk away from the crash unchanged.

I walked away reborn.

CHAPTER 5 — Between Life and Death

There is a space the body enters before it knows whether it will stay or go—a space suspended between breath and stillness, between heartbeat and silence. It isn't life, but it isn't death either. It's something else entirely. Something sacred. Something wordless. Something that changes you forever.

I didn't know such a place existed until the crash brought me there.

I wasn't unconscious, yet I wasn't fully present. It felt as if the physical world had blurred, leaving me hovering somewhere just above it. I could sense my body, but I wasn't trapped inside it. I could hear the world, but it sounded far away. Everything heavy became weightless. Everything loud became muted. Everything frightening became strangely calm.

It was like standing between two doors—one leading forward, one leading beyond—and for the first time, I felt no fear of either.

In that suspended in-between, I didn't feel pain. I didn't feel panic. What I felt was clarity—a clarity so sharp and so gentle at the same time that it felt almost divine. My mind, which had always been loud and layered and full of spiraling thoughts, became quiet. Quiet in a way I had never experienced before. Quiet in a way that felt like the truth.

I realized in that moment that I had lived so much of my life carrying noise that wasn't mine. Emotions that weren't mine. Expectations that weren't mine. I had held on to weight I thought was normal simply because I had gotten used to carrying it. But when everything inside me went still, I felt what it was like to be…free.

A freedom so unfamiliar it almost felt like someone else's life.

I saw myself clearly for the first time—not the version of me shaped by other people's needs or my own fears, but the raw, unfiltered self underneath it all. The self I had prayed for without fully understanding. The self I had asked God to help me align with. The self I had always been growing toward without noticing.

It amazed me how much truth can fit inside a single silent moment.

As I floated there, between life and death, I felt gratitude. Real, deep gratitude. Gratitude for the life I had lived so far. Gratitude for the people who had shaped me. Gratitude even for the pain, because it had carved out the space for the strength I didn't know I had.

More than anything, I felt purpose.

Not the kind you chase, not the kind you analyze, not the kind you try to control—but the kind that simply is. The kind that exists deep in your bones. The kind that wakes up with you and belongs to you even when you forget it's there.

I realized I wasn't afraid of dying. I was afraid of not having lived aligned with the person I truly was. And in that suspended space, I knew I had one more life to live—the real one. The aligned one. The purposeful one.

The one that was waiting for me on the other side of this moment.

I thought about how I had always felt things so deeply, how I could read people without trying, how I could sense emotions that were never spoken. For so long, I believed that meant I was "too much." Too emotional. Too sensitive. Too observant. But in that in-between space, I realized something:

That was never a flaw.
It was a gift.
A guidance system.
A calling.

Every thought felt like it had been filtered through truth. Every feeling made sense. Every memory aligned into a single understanding: nothing in my life had been random. Every lesson, every pain, every shift, every whisper had been preparing me for something greater.

I wasn't being punished.
I wasn't being tested.
I was being awakened.

This space between life and death wasn't meant to take me—it was meant to show me. It was a mirror held up to my soul, letting me see everything I had been blind to in the rush of everyday life.

I understood then that perspectives are never permanent. They change as we grow. They expand as we shed old versions of ourselves. The only thing that remains unchanged is the past—but even that loses its weight when we stop carrying it into the future.

There in the quiet, I felt myself release all the things that had once consumed me:

The fear.
The doubt.
Overthinking.
The heaviness that didn't belong to me.
The versions of myself I had outgrown.

I let them all fall away like dead leaves.

And in their place, something else bloomed—an understanding so simple and powerful it softened everything inside me:

"There is nothing for me to be sorry about. I am alive. I am grateful. I am blessed. And I am ready to live differently."

I didn't return to my body in panic.
I returned with purpose.

I didn't return confused.
I returned home.

I didn't return broken.
I returned whole in a way I had never been.

When my spirit settled fully back inside me, I opened my eyes not into the life I had lived before—but into a new one. A second life. A life that had been waiting for me to step into it with clarity, discipline, and peace.

The space between life and death didn't take me.

It transformed me.

CHAPTER 6 — Waking Up in a New Life

Waking up after the crash felt nothing like returning to the same world. It felt like opening my eyes for the very first time. The air felt different. My body felt lighter. Even the colors around me seemed sharper, as if someone had quietly turned the clarity of my life all the way up while I wasn't watching.

Survival wasn't a miracle.
Awareness was.
Transformation was.
Alignment was.

My body was intact, but my spirit had taken a new shape. It moved differently inside me—calmer, wiser, more grounded than I had ever known myself to be. I wasn't waking up into fear or confusion. I didn't ask, Why did this happen to me?

Instead, the only words that rose in me were:
What now?

There was no bitterness, no anger, no resentment trying to pull me under. If anything, resentment felt impossible. I knew instantly that if I allowed even a small seed of negative emotion to settle inside me, it would grow roots and poison everything this moment had given me. So I made a decision the moment I regained consciousness:

I would not resent the crash.
Not a single part of it.

Because what happened that day didn't break me—it revealed me. It released me. It delivered me into the life I was actually meant to live.

I became protective of my thoughts in a way I never had before. Not out of fear, but out of discipline. I understood now how powerful the mind was. How easily negativity could become a virus if left unattended. I chose to guard my inner world with intention, not because I was avoiding pain, but because I finally knew my purpose deserved clarity.

Every day after the crash felt like an invitation to live, not just exist. I noticed everything I had once rushed past—the way sunlight hit surfaces, the pattern of breaths people took when they were about to speak, the vibrations of energy in a room, even my own heartbeat. I felt connected to life in a way that was almost startling.

I realized something simple and profound:
Every day is an opportunity to grow and appreciate the life you are given.

Not in a cliché way. Not in a "be positive" way. But in a deeply conscious way—one where gratitude becomes instinct, not effort. My stress, my anxiety, my urge to control everything... they all dissolved. Not because I ignored them, but because they no longer had a place in the world I stepped into.

The more I let go of my attachment to outcomes, the more life opened itself to me. I stopped gripping everything so tightly. I stopped trying to force things to make sense. I stopped chasing clarity from a place of fear.

And the moment I released control, I gained alignment.

What was meant for me began moving toward me without resistance. What wasn't meant for me drifted away with gentle finality. I didn't feel panic when something didn't work out. I didn't feel disappointed when plans changed. I understood that a closed path wasn't rejection—it was redirection.

The present moment became enough.
The present version of me became enough.

This didn't happen instantly. Healing never does. It wasn't like flipping a switch—it was like opening a door and walking through it a little more each day. But every step felt guided. Every step felt intentional. Every step felt like confirmation that I had been given another chance, not just to live, but to live aligned.

I noticed, too, that my energy was changing the people around me. Not because I said anything profound, but because alignment is contagious. Peace is contagious. When you stop holding onto fear, others feel safer around you. When you let go of negativity, others naturally soften. When you walk with purpose, others rise to meet their own.

People began opening up to me more. They trusted me faster. They gravitated toward me without knowing why. They felt something in me that was different—something they couldn't name but could feel.

I realized then that my transformation wasn't meant to stay with me.
It was meant to move through me.
It was meant to guide others.
It was meant to ripple out into the world in ways I didn't even have to try for.

I had been saved, not just for my own journey, but to become a mirror for others—to show what alignment looks like, feels like, and creates.

Waking up after the crash wasn't the end of the story.
It was the beginning of the real one.

The life I lived before had been preparing me.
The moment between life and death had awakened me.

And this—this new life—was where the transformation would take root.

I didn't wake up afraid of dying.
I woke up determined to live.

And for the first time ever, I finally understood what that meant.

CHAPTER 7 — The Silence After Survival

The hours after the crash felt unreal—too quiet, too slow, too heavy in a way that didn't suffocate me, but reshaped me. It was a silence that didn't belong to the world outside; it belonged to something inside me. The kind of silence that only comes after life has shown you the thin line between existence and eternity.

It wasn't the kind of silence that follows shock.
It was the silence that followed revelation.

The world around me moved strangely—like everything was continuing at its regular pace, but I was observing it from a few steps deeper. Colors looked the same, but they meant something different. Sounds echoed inside me instead of just around me. Time lost its usual texture. And for the first time in a long time, I was fully aware of my own breathing.

I wasn't thinking about the crash anymore. I wasn't replaying it or trying to make sense of it. I wasn't trying to understand how I survived. Instead, I was trying to understand who I was now.

There is a moment after survival where you are alive, but not fully returned. Your body is in this world, but your spirit is still standing on the threshold of the one it just visited. I felt split—one part of me grounded, the other still floating in the clarity I had touched between life and death.

Everything felt fragile and profound at the same time.

People talk about adrenaline. They talk about panic. They talk about the physical aftermath of near-death experiences. But no one talks about the quiet. No one talks about the strange, heavy stillness that settles into your bones when you realize life just gave you back to yourself.

It's not a relief.
It's not fear.
It's a realization.

Realization that your life could've ended—but didn't.
Realization that you are now responsible for the second chance you've been given.
Realization that you cannot go back to who you were before, no matter how familiar that version of you felt.

I could feel the shift in places I didn't have words for.

My senses were heightened.
My intuition felt louder.
My emotions felt deeper but calmer.
My thoughts moved slower and sharper, like each one was filtered through purpose.

I noticed details I would've ignored before—the tremble in someone's voice, the way light flickered when someone's energy shifted, the way my own body responded to the presence of others. Everything was data, and I absorbed it without effort, like my spirit suddenly knew how to read the world with new eyes.

But with awareness came weight.
Not a heavy weight—an intentional one.

I realized how carelessly I had moved through life before. Not reckless, just... unaware. Unaware of how precious time was. Unaware of how meaningful the smallest interactions could be. Unaware of my own spiritual responsibility.

There was a moment later that day where I sat alone—no noise, no distractions, no one asking if I was okay—and I felt the silence settle around me like a blanket. It wasn't comforting, and it wasn't frightening. It was revealing.

It revealed everything I had been avoiding.
Everything I had been carrying.
Everything I had been meant to become.

I wasn't the same girl who got into the car that morning.
I wasn't the same girl who prayed the night before.
I wasn't even the same girl who cried, laughed, healed, or broke in the years leading up to that moment.

I had crossed a threshold.
And crossing it meant I would never be able to fit back into the old version of my life.

People talk about a "new chapter."
But this wasn't a new chapter.
This was a new book entirely.

I didn't suddenly understand everything.
I didn't have a roadmap.
I didn't know what was coming next.

But I knew this:

I had been awakened.
And awakenings do not let you return to sleep.

The silence after survival wasn't emptiness.
It was space—space for the truth to echo.
Space for the old self to fall away.
Space for the new self to breathe for the first time.

It was in that silence that I realized:

I was not saved to return to who I was.
I was saved to become who I was meant to be.

And the journey into that version of myself was only beginning.

CHAPTER 8 — Walking With New Eyes

In the days that followed the crash, I moved through the world as if I had been given a new pair of eyes—eyes that didn't just look, but saw. Everything felt sharper, clearer, more intentional. It was as though life had peeled away a layer of fog I never realized I'd been living behind.

I didn't rush anymore.
I didn't drift.
I didn't move on autopilot.

Each step felt guided.
Each thought felt deliberate.
Each moment felt like it carried a message.

I didn't ask for this new sense of awareness—it simply arrived with the breath I took when I woke up alive. And once it settled in me, I knew I could never go back to seeing the world the way I once did.

Walking with new eyes isn't just about observing life differently.
It's about feeling life differently.

I began noticing small things that once blended into the background: the way someone shifted their weight when they were holding back a truth, the way a room's energy changed when someone walked in with a burden, the way my own heartbeat synced with clarity when I listened to my intuition instead of my fear.

It felt like stepping into a new dimension of awareness—one that had always been available to me, but one I had never slowed down long enough to enter.

People looked different too.
Not physically—but energetically.

I could sense who was hurting without them saying a word.
I could feel when someone wasn't aligned with their own life.
I could tell when someone was carrying weight that didn't belong
to them.

It wasn't judgment.
It wasn't analysis.
It was recognition.

When your eyes change, your understanding deepens.

I began to realize how many people walk through life
spiritually asleep, carrying burdens that aren't theirs, ignoring signs
that are meant for them, calling their pain "normal" because
they've never known anything else. I recognized it because I had
been one of them.

And with that awareness came a strange sense of
responsibility—not to fix people, not to save them, but to see
them. Truly see them in a world where most people barely see
themselves.

My intuition, once a quiet whisper I doubted, had grown
louder—clearer—almost impossible to ignore. It wasn't dramatic.
It wasn't mystical. It was knowing. A guiding presence inside me
that felt older than my physical life. A compass pointing me toward
what—and who—I was meant to encounter.

Signs showed up everywhere, woven into the fabric of my days
like patterns on a tapestry:

A certain number appears again and again.
A song that played at the exact moment my mind wandered to a
specific memory.

A person looking at me as if they sensed something different.
A sudden pull in my chest that told me when to step closer—or step away.

Before the crash, I would've brushed these things off.
After the crash, they felt like instructions.
Or reminders.
Or confirmations that I wasn't walking blindly anymore.

Walking with new eyes felt like walking with God—not beside me, but within me. In my attention. In my awareness. In my stillness.

I realized something profound during this time:
Awakening doesn't just change what you see.
It changes what you can't ignore anymore.

I could no longer ignore my calling.
I could no longer ignore misaligned relationships.
I could no longer ignore the heaviness I used to carry out of habit.
I could no longer ignore the truth of who I was meant to become.

Life became louder in its signals and quieter in its chaos.
People became more complex and more transparent at the same time.
The world felt both bigger and smaller—bigger in its meaning, smaller in its distractions.

Because once you awaken, distractions lose their power.

I didn't feel detached from the world.
I felt deeply connected to it—just not controlled by it anymore.

Walking with new eyes was a blessing, but it also came with adjustment. I had to learn how to navigate life with heightened sensitivity, with deeper intuition, with a spirit that no longer tolerated what it used to. I learned to listen more and explain less. I learned to observe without absorbing. I learned to trust the pull inside me even when it didn't make sense.

This wasn't about figuring everything out.
It was about honoring what I now saw.
About honoring clarity.
About honoring the second chance I had been given.

Because once your eyes open—truly open—you realize that everything before was preparation.

And everything ahead has a purpose.

CHAPTER 9 — The Weight People Carry

Once my eyes opened to the world in a new way, I began to see something I had sensed all my life but never fully understood: people carry weight they were never meant to hold. Weight that settles into their shoulders, their posture, their voice, their energy. Weight that shapes the way they move through life, even when they pretend they're fine.

I didn't just see this weight — I could feel it.

Walking into a room, I could sense who was drowning beneath invisible burdens. Looking into someone's eyes, I could see the heaviness they tried to hide. Standing next to someone, I could feel the tension they carried in their spirit, the exhaustion they camouflaged behind a smile.

It wasn't something I searched for.
It was something I recognized.

Because before the crash, I had carried weight that wasn't mine too.

I had carried expectations placed on me by people who didn't understand me.
I had carried pain that belonged to others because I didn't want them to carry it alone.
I had carried fears projected onto me by those who didn't know any better.
I had carried disappointment that never belonged to my journey.

I didn't know back then that empathy, when unguarded, becomes a magnet for other people's shadows.

But now—I saw it clearly.

The world is full of people quietly carrying demons they didn't create, battles they didn't choose, and burdens they didn't earn. And most of them don't even know they can put them down.

It became impossible for me to look at someone and only see their surface. My vision went deeper now—past the words, past the body language, past the practiced expressions. I saw the stories in their silence. I saw their unspoken hurts. I saw the moments that shaped them into who they had become.

It didn't overwhelm me the way it once did.
The crash had changed that too.

Now, instead of absorbing their weight, I observed it.
Instead of carrying their pain, I recognized it.
Instead of letting their heaviness drown me, I learned to stay afloat.

Because awakening doesn't just teach you to see others.
It teaches you to protect yourself while doing it.

But even with boundaries, I couldn't ignore what I saw.

I saw the mother who carried the weight of being strong for everyone but herself.
The friend who joked too much so no one would see her breaking.
The man who held himself together with silence because he didn't know how to ask for help.
The young girl who carried the weight of her family's expectations on shoulders too small.
The people who buried themselves in work because it was easier than facing their own reflection.

And every single one of them thought they were alone.

But they weren't.
No one is.

Most people just need someone to see them—not fix them, not judge them, not analyze them, but see them. And for reasons I didn't fully understand yet, life kept placing me in front of people who needed exactly that.

I became aware of how often people walk through life holding things they never question. Pain passed down from generations. Guilt inherited from parents. Roles assigned to them before they knew themselves. And because no one teaches them how to let go, they learn to survive under the weight instead of setting it down.

This awakening wasn't about offering solutions.
It was about understanding the truth:

Not all weight is yours to carry.
Not all pain is yours to hold.
Not all energy is yours to absorb.

And most importantly—
Not every burden you see needs to become yours.

Awareness gave me clarity.
Clarity gave me compassion.
Compassion gave me discernment.

I learned to separate what belonged to me from what didn't.
I learned to let others carry what is theirs without losing myself in the process.
I learned the difference between supporting someone and sacrificing myself for them.

But even with boundaries, I couldn't shake this new understanding:

Everyone is carrying something.
And most people have no idea how heavy it truly is.

This realization didn't make me sad—it made me present.
It made me intentional.
It made me available in a way that didn't drain me anymore.

Instead of being consumed by their heaviness, I became grounded in my own light.

The crash didn't just open my eyes—it opened my heart in a way that allowed me to see people with more depth, more compassion, and more honesty than ever before.

Because once you know what it feels like to almost lose your life, you begin to recognize how many people are losing themselves while still breathing.

And that knowledge changed the way I walked through the world forever.

CHAPTER 10 — The Man in the Parking Lot

It happened on an evening that should've been forgettable. A simple moment in an ordinary day — the kind you barely pay attention to. I was sitting in a parking lot, trying to decide where I wanted to eat, lost in the small indecision that fills the quiet spaces of life.

The world around me felt still.
Not silent — still.
Like time had slowed down just enough for something to slip through.

That was when I saw him.

A man walking across the lot, moving without direction but with a heaviness that seemed stitched into his steps. He looked confused, weighed down, almost suffocated by something no one else could see. But I saw it. Not with my eyes — with the same spiritual sight that had awakened in me since the crash.

His weight wasn't physical.
It wasn't situational.
It wasn't even his.

He was chained to something that didn't belong to him — someone else's demons, someone else's pain, someone else's expectations. I recognized it instantly because I had carried weight like that before. I knew what it looked like when a soul moved under a burden it was never meant to hold.

Most people would've looked away.
Most people do — not out of cruelty, but because seeing someone clearly means feeling them too.

But I didn't look away.
I couldn't.

Something in my spirit leaned toward him, as if the air itself had nudged me.

He walked up to me hesitantly, careful, almost apologetic. When he reached my window, he didn't ask for much — just a dollar. His voice was soft, polite, almost embarrassed.

And the old me might've said no.
Not out of judgment.
Not out of fear.
Simply out of the habit of protecting myself from the unknown.

But the awakened me — the aligned me — saw a soul in need, not a man asking for money.

And I knew instantly that this moment wasn't random.
I was meant to be here.
He was meant to cross my path.
Something bigger was orchestrating this.

I didn't have any cash on me. Normally, that would've been the end of it. But my spirit was louder than my logic that night. I looked at him and said, "Wait here. I'll be right back."

He seemed surprised that I didn't dismiss him. Surprised that I didn't shrink away. Surprised that I didn't treat him like a problem or a threat. I saw that shock in his eyes — the shock of being seen as a human being instead of a burden.

There was an ATM nearby, and I walked toward it with complete certainty. I wasn't thinking. I wasn't calculating. I wasn't reconsidering. Something within me was guiding me, and I trusted it without hesitation.

I withdrew forty dollars.
Not one dollar.
Not five.
Forty.

When I walked back, I handed him a twenty — nineteen times what he had asked for. His face changed instantly. Surprise. Confusion. Gratitude layered with disbelief. He looked at the bill as if it couldn't possibly be real.

But I wasn't done.

I looked him in the eyes and said words that didn't come from thought — they came from something deeper, something older, something wiser inside me:

"Bless your soul. Bless your family, your loved ones, your future, your present, and your past. This money is not my business once it leaves my hands. But what you do with it will shape your life. Don't let it chain you deeper to a burden that was never yours."

He stared at me like no one had ever spoken to him that way before.

I wasn't trying to be profound.
I wasn't trying to be a savior.
I wasn't trying to make a moment.

I was simply honoring what my spirit told me to do.

Because that night, I didn't just see him in reality. I saw him in spirit.
I saw the light in him buried under layers of weight.
I saw the soul trying to break free.
I saw the angel in him trapped beneath someone else's suffering.

And I couldn't ignore that.

He thanked me more times than I can remember. His voice shook. His eyes softened. But what touched me most wasn't his gratitude — it was the shift in his energy. The heaviness he carried didn't disappear, but it loosened. It cracked. It moved.

I drove away without expecting anything. I didn't consider the moment heroic. I didn't tell anyone about it. I didn't even fully understand what had happened until later.

But over the next few weeks, I saw him again — not in the same place, not in the same condition, but in existence.

His entire aura had changed.
He was standing taller.
He was moving with purpose.
His spirit felt freer, lighter, almost glowing with something new.

And every time I saw him, I felt confirmation echo through me:

"When someone asks for one, give them nineteen more."

Not literally — spiritually.

Give them more compassion.
More understanding.
More patience.
More hope.
More humanity.
More love.

The world gives so little.
So little grace.
So little kindness.
So little space for people to breathe.

But I learned something that night in the parking lot:

Sometimes your purpose is not to change someone's entire life.
Sometimes your purpose is to change one moment.
And one moment is enough.

The man who once walked burdened now walked blessed —
not because of the money, but because someone finally saw him
without judgment, without fear, without conditions.

And in seeing him, I saw another layer of my own awakening.

My purpose wasn't just to survive.
It was to serve.
To guide.
To witness.
To bless.
To pour into others in ways the world never poured into me.

This encounter was not an accident.
It was an alignment.
It was confirmation.
It was the universe saying:

"You are becoming who you were meant to be."

CHAPTER 11 — Giving More Than You're Asked For

That night in the parking lot stayed with me long after the moment passed. Not because I gave someone money, but because of what the moment revealed. What it confirmed. What it awakened inside me.

Most people think generosity is about the amount you give.
But real generosity is spiritual, not material.
It's not about the money — it's about the intention.
It's about the energy behind the act.

When I handed that man more than he asked for, something shifted in me. I felt it immediately — like something old had broken open, and something new had quietly taken its place.

Because giving is not about filling someone's hands.
It's about filling the space where their hope has been dying.

When he asked for a dollar, he wasn't just asking for money.
He was asking to be seen.
To be acknowledged.
To be treated like a human being.
To be spoken to with dignity instead of fear or judgment.

He was asking for a moment of relief in a world that had been unkind to him.

And something in my spirit knew that giving him the bare minimum would only repeat the same patterns he had always known: scarcity, dismissal, being tolerated instead of valued.

But alignment — real alignment — demands more of you.

It asks you to show up differently.
To give differently.
To love differently.

It asks you to respond from your spirit, not your logic.

And that night, my spirit led.

The lesson became clear only afterward, when life had given me enough quiet to understand it:

When someone asks for one, give them nineteen more.
Not always in money — though sometimes yes.
But in patience.
In kindness.
In understanding.
In gentleness.
In compassion.
In presence.

The world teaches people to give the bare minimum.
Spiritual alignment teaches you to give from overflow.

Not to drain yourself.
Not to save everyone.
Not to be responsible for every soul you meet.

But to recognize when you are in the presence of a divine moment — a moment where you are meant to pour into someone because they no longer have the strength to pour into themselves.

Giving "nineteen more" doesn't mean losing pieces of yourself.
It means giving from the part of you that is connected to something bigger.

Because abundance is not about how much you have.
Abundance is about how much you are willing to circulate.

How much trust you have in life's ability to return to you what you give away freely.

That night taught me something sacred:

When the universe places someone in front of you, it is rarely random.
Humans intersect for reasons.
Souls collide with purpose.
Paths cross with intention.

You don't have to fix everyone.
You don't have to solve their lives.
You don't have to carry their pain.

But when you have the opportunity to lighten someone's weight — even for a moment — you are honoring the very reason you survived.

The man in the parking lot didn't just receive money.
He received a message.
A blessing.
A reflection of his worthiness.
A reminder that his life still held value, that he wasn't invisible, that someone believed in him even if only for a moment.

And sometimes, that's all a person needs to shift their entire direction.

What struck me most was what happened afterward — seeing him again, not by coincidence but by confirmation. His spirit had changed. His presence had changed. There was a spark in him where there had been darkness. A lift where there had been drag. A sense of purpose where there had been confusion.

And that taught me something even deeper:

The impact you have on someone may never be measured by the moment — it may be measured by who they become after it.

That encounter left a permanent imprint on my journey. It sharpened my intuition. It amplified my calling. It showed me that my presence, my awareness, my energy had the power to alter the course of another person's day, or even their life.

Not because I'm special.
But because I am aligned.
Because I listen.
Because I trust the pull in my spirit when it speaks.

Giving more than you're asked for is not about excess.
It's about intention.

It's about choosing to be a vessel when the universe needs one.
It's about responding from your soul, not your scarcity.
It's about understanding that blessings multiply when they are shared.

That night, I didn't give money.

I gave hope.

And in return, I received confirmation:

My purpose wasn't to survive the crash.
My purpose was to live in alignment with the person who walked out of it.

CHAPTER 13 — Shedding the Old Self

Awakening doesn't happen all at once.
It isn't a single moment or a clear line you cross.
It is a shedding — slow, deliberate, sometimes painful, always necessary.

After the crash, after the clarity, after the growing awareness of my calling, I began to realize something I had never fully understood:

I could not step into who I was meant to be…
while still carrying who I used to be.

There is a weight that comes from holding onto outdated versions of yourself — versions built from survival, from fear, from pleasing others, from misunderstanding your worth. Those versions feel familiar, but they are heavy. They take up space meant for growth. They keep you tied to places you've already outgrown.

And for the first time in my life, I felt the full truth of that weight.

I didn't feel guilty.
I didn't feel sad.
I didn't feel nostalgic.

I felt ready.

Ready to release the identities I had worn for too long.
Ready to let go of the expectations that weren't mine.
Ready to step away from energy that no longer resonated with my spirit.
Ready to allow the old versions of me to die so the new one could breathe.

The shedding began quietly.

I started noticing when I felt out of alignment.
I started hearing my intuition louder than my fear.
I started feeling discomfort in spaces I once tolerated.
I started drifting away from people whose presence felt dim instead of light.

This wasn't isolation — it was transformation.

The old version of me had been built on weight.
The new version of me was being built on truth.

I had to confront parts of myself I didn't realize were still clinging to me:

The part of me that stayed quiet to avoid conflict.
The part of me that cared too deeply about being understood.
The part of me that took responsibility for emotions that weren't mine.
The part of me that carried guilt for choosing myself.
The part of me that apologized for simply existing in my fullness.

These parts weren't bad.
They were just outdated.
They belonged to a version of me that didn't survive the crash — a version that needed to be honored, thanked, and released.

Because growth requires mourning the versions of yourself you no longer are.

There were moments when the shedding felt confusing.
Moments when I didn't recognize myself at first.
Moments when I wondered if I was becoming too distant, too direct, too aware.

But awakening wasn't making me someone else —
it was returning me to myself.

I began to understand boundaries, not as walls, but as sacred spaces that protected my spirit. I learned that saying "no" was not rejection; it was alignment. I learned that choosing myself did not harm others; it healed me.

And I learned something even more profound:

Some people are attached to your unhealed self.
They only understand you in your past form.
When you shed that version, they don't know how to relate to you anymore.

Some drifted away quietly.
Some resisted the change.
Some tried to pull me back into patterns I had already outgrown.
Some projected their discomfort onto me.

But none of that stopped what was happening inside me.

Because once purpose enters you — truly enters you — you cannot shrink yourself back into who you were before.

I felt myself becoming stronger.
Sharper.
Softer in some ways, firmer in others.
More intuitive.
More intentional.
More aligned.

I was stepping into the version of me I had prayed for — the version that stood in truth without apology. The version that could see through people without absorbing their pain. The version that understood that peace is not found in avoiding life, but in living it honestly.

Letting go of the old self wasn't a rejection of my past — it was a graduation from it.

I honored the girl I used to be.
I thanked her for surviving.
I thanked her for carrying the weight until I was ready to put it down.
I thanked her for doing the best she could with what she knew at the time.

But she wasn't meant to walk with me into this life.

This new version — the aligned version — required space to breathe.
Space to expand.
Space to rise.

Shedding the old self is not about loss.
It is about liberation.

And standing there, in the quiet aftermath of rebirth, I finally understood:

The crash didn't take anything from me.
It freed me from everything that was never mine to hold.

CHAPTER 14 — Becoming the Aligned Self

Alignment. Not a moment.
A becoming.

It is the slow, steady merging of who you are with who you are meant to be.
It is the unraveling of everything false and the rising of everything true.
It is choosing yourself without apology, without hesitation, without shrinking.

After shedding the parts of me that no longer belonged, I began to step fully into the version of myself that had been waiting for years — the aligned self. The one who didn't just survive life, but understood it. The one who didn't just feel deeply, but navigated that depth with clarity instead of drowning in it.

This version of me didn't appear suddenly.
She revealed herself piece by piece.

Through small moments.
Through instinct.
Through choices that felt like truth instead of fear.

The aligned self isn't perfect — she is aware.
She isn't loud — she is clear.
She isn't forceful — she is certain.

I began waking up each day with a new kind of purpose, one that wasn't tied to tasks or outcomes or achievements. It was tied to presence. To intention. To listen inward before responding outward.

Life started to feel synchronized, as if everything was happening with meaning, not coincidence. Conversations aligned with thoughts I had earlier that day. Opportunities showed up in moments when my spirit felt ready. Encounters felt destined. Lessons repeated until I embodied them.

And I realized something profound:

Alignment feels like coming home to yourself.

I no longer questioned my intuition — I trusted it.
I no longer carried guilt for choosing myself — I embraced it.
I no longer allowed fear to shape my decisions — I released it.
I no longer tried to convince people to understand me — I walked in my truth regardless.

There is a confidence that grows when you step into alignment. Not ego. Not arrogance. A quiet, grounded confidence that comes from finally living as the person your soul recognizes.

The aligned self knows:

When to speak and when to stay still.
When to hold on and when to let go.
When to act and when to trust the unfolding.
When something is meant for her — and when it isn't.

I started to notice the way my spirit responded to different spaces and different people. Some environments made me feel expansive. Others made me shrink. Some people felt like sunlight. Others felt like storms waiting to happen. My body knew before my mind did.

Alignment taught me to listen to those signals.

Because your body is the first messenger of your soul.

The more I honored those messages, the stronger they became.
The more I followed my instincts, the more aligned my life became.
The more I trusted the path unfolding beneath me, the easier it was to let go of what resisted.

I didn't need validation anymore.
I didn't need permission.
I didn't need reassurance.

I had myself — truly, finally, fully.

And that changed everything.

Alignment softened me where I had been hardened.
It strengthened me where I had been fragile.
It illuminated me where I once felt dim.
It anchored me where I once felt lost.

People noticed the shift — even those who couldn't describe it. They'd tell me I felt different. Calmer. Stronger. More grounded. They didn't know how to explain it, but they could feel the difference.

That's what alignment does — it speaks before you do.

It radiates from your presence.
It vibrates in your voice.
It shows in your choices.
It echoes in the way others feel when they are around you.

The aligned self is magnetic — not because she tries to be, but because she exists in truth.

And truth is irresistible to those who have forgotten their own.

This chapter of my life wasn't about discovering who I was.
It was about becoming her.
Choosing her.
Honoring her.
Listening to her.

I realized that alignment doesn't demand perfection — it demands honesty.
Honesty with yourself.
Honesty with your spirit.
Honesty with the path life is calling you toward.

And the deeper I leaned into this version of myself, the clearer it became:

I was not just surviving my awakening.
I was stepping into the woman I was shaped to be.

CHAPTER 15 — Relationships Through New Eyes

When you awaken, you don't just see yourself differently.
You see everyone differently.

You begin to notice the truth behind people's words, the intentions beneath their actions, and the energy that follows them like a second shadow. You start recognizing who nourishes your spirit and who drains it. Who aligns with your growth and who only aligns with your old wounds.

Awakening doesn't end your relationships.
It reveals them.

It shows you who was walking with you, and who was simply standing next to you.
Who loved you deeply, and who loved the version of you that didn't know her worth.
Who grew with you, and who only grew comfortable with your silence.

For a while, this realization hurt.

Not because I lost people, but because I outgrew versions of myself that their presence depended on.

I began to see the patterns — the emotional roles I had unknowingly played:

The one who stayed quiet to keep the peace.
The one who held pain so others didn't have to feel it.
The one who forgave too quickly.
The one who dimmed her intuitive voice to avoid intimidating others.

The one who showed up fully for people who only showed up halfway.

Awakening forced me to see the truth:

I had been loyal to people who were never loyal to my growth.
I had been present for people who disappeared when I needed them.
I had been understanding toward people who never tried to understand me.

And for the first time, I wasn't willing to repeat those patterns.

Because alignment requires honesty — even when it's uncomfortable.

I started noticing which relationships felt peaceful, and which felt heavy. Which conversations expanded me, and which drained me. Which people supported the woman I was becoming, and which ones depended on the woman I had been.

Some connections naturally deepened — the ones built on truth, mutual respect, shared growth. These relationships felt lighter now, freer, more sacred. They met me where I was without asking me to shrink. They saw my transformation not as a threat, but as an invitation.

But others... fell away.

Some quietly faded.
Some broke open.
Some simply no longer felt aligned.

Not because they were bad or wrong, but because we no longer resonated on the same frequency. Awakening changes the wavelength at which your spirit vibrates, and not everyone is able — or willing — to rise with you.

For a while, I tried to hold on. I tried to explain, to soften the shift, to reassure people that I was still "me." But the truth was, I wasn't. And pretending only created tension inside my spirit.

At some point, I realized:

The people meant for your aligned self won't require you to return to your unaligned version.

And with that clarity came peace.

I stopped forcing conversations that didn't nourish me.
I stopped seeking validation from people who couldn't see my growth.
I stopped entertaining energy that felt chaotic or draining.
I stopped apologizing for the boundaries that protected my spirit.

I didn't lose relationships because I woke up.
I simply outgrew the ones that couldn't expand with me.

And those who remained — those who matched my energy, my growth, my alignment — became even more sacred. These were the people who met me at depth, who understood my silence, who honored my transformation, who held space for my becoming.

But perhaps the biggest transformation was this:

For the first time in my life, my relationship with myself became the priority.

I began choosing myself without guilt.
I began protecting my peace without explanation.
I began trusting my instincts without fear.
I began loving myself in a way that didn't depend on who stayed or who left.

My relationships didn't define me anymore.
My alignment did.

And as I grew deeper into this truth, something beautiful happened:

I no longer needed people to understand my journey — I simply needed them to respect it.

Some did.
Some didn't.
But either way, I kept walking.

Because awakening taught me this:

People come into your life for different reasons —
to grow you, to teach you, to challenge you, to love you, or to prepare you.

But not all of them are meant to stay.

The ones who are meant for your aligned self will rise with you.
The others will fall away — not as a loss, but as a clearing.

A clearing that makes room for deeper love, deeper connection, deeper truth.

A clearing that makes room for the people who will walk beside the version of you that has awakened.

A clearing that makes space for the life that is waiting for you.

CHAPTER 16 — The Art of Seeing Souls

There are gifts in this world that can be taught.
And then there are gifts that are born into you.

Seeing souls — really seeing them — is one of those gifts.

Long before the crash, long before the awakening, long before
I understood myself, this ability lived quietly within me. I felt
people before I heard them. I understood emotions before they
were spoken. I sensed truths before they were revealed.

But I didn't know what to do with it.
I didn't know how to hold it.
I didn't know how to separate what belonged to me from what
belonged to others.

So I carried everything — the joy, the pain, the fear, the
heaviness of people who had never learned how to carry
themselves. I took it all in like a sponge, unaware that my empathy
was swallowing me whole.

But awakening didn't give me this gift —
It gave me clarity about it.

It taught me the difference between burden and purpose.
Between absorbing and understanding.
Between carrying someone and guiding someone.

After the crash, my intuition sharpened in a way that felt
almost supernatural.
I didn't just sense emotions — I saw them.
I didn't just hear words — I read the energy that lived beneath
them.
I didn't just witness people — I understood them on a level they
didn't understand themselves yet.

This was not judgment.
It was recognition.

A deep, spiritual recognition of the truth someone's soul was trying to speak, even when their mind was drowning it out.

I started seeing patterns:

Some people speak from their wounds.
Some from their fear.
Some from their ego.
Some from their longing.
Some from the small child within them who never got to grow safely.

And I could see all of it — instantly.

There were moments when I looked at someone and saw the weight they were dragging behind them. Not physically, but energetically. The chains of old heartbreak. The shadow of past trauma. The echoes of unspoken guilt. The exhaustion of pretending everything was fine.

Before, these insights overwhelmed me.
Now, they grounded me.

I learned to observe without absorbing.
To understand without inheriting.
To feel without losing myself.

This is the art of seeing souls —
a balance of intuition and self-protection.

The moment I started honoring this gift, my life changed:

I attracted people who were searching for clarity.
I encountered strangers who felt drawn to open up.

I guided conversations without forcing them.
I offered healing without claiming ownership of anyone's journey.

People often think that being intuitive means reading minds.
But it's deeper than that.

It means hearing the emotions someone swallowed.
It means seeing the truth behind their smile.
It means recognizing the version of them they have forgotten.
It means feeling the storm before it becomes thunder in their life.

And the more I leaned into this gift, the more intentional I became about protecting it.

Because not everyone deserves access to a "soul".
Not everyone respects emotional insight.
Not everyone is ready to be seen.

I learned to set boundaries — boundaries that honored my energy and prevented me from drowning in the emotional waters of others.

Seeing souls doesn't mean saving them.
It means acknowledging their truth with compassion.
It means reflecting what they've been afraid to admit.
It means offering light, not carrying their darkness.

The parking lot encounter was one example of this gift working through me.
But there were countless others — small interactions that left people lighter, simply because someone finally saw them.

For the first time, I understood:

My gift wasn't random.
It wasn't overwhelming.
It wasn't "too much."

It was for a purpose.

Purpose that came with responsibility.
Purpose that came with clarity.
Purpose that came with a calling.

Seeing souls is not a task — it is a presence.
It is the quiet confidence of knowing that you don't need to fix
people to change them.
Sometimes, all you need to do is witness them without judgment.

That witnessing alone becomes healing.

Because most people are not broken —
they are unseen.

And when someone finally sees them, truly sees them, they
remember themselves.
They remember their worth.
They remember their strength.

Awakening taught me how to use this gift with intention
instead of fear.
It taught me how to protect myself while guiding others.
How to stay grounded while reading energy.
How to lead without forcing.

And perhaps most importantly:

It taught me that the ability to see souls is not about insight —
It is about love.

The pure kind.
The unconditional kind.
The kind that recognizes the divine in every human being, even
when life has tried to bury it.

This gift is no longer something I carry quietly.
It is something I honor.
Something I use with purpose.
Something I understand now as one of the reasons I survived.

CHAPTER 17 — You Were Saved to Lead

There comes a moment in every awakening when you realize that everything you survived, everything you learned, everything you transformed wasn't just for you. It wasn't just meant to heal you, or guide you, or strengthen you. It was meant to prepare you.

Prepare you to lead.

The realization didn't hit me all at once.
It unfolded slowly, like a sunrise — gentle at first, then impossible to ignore.
I started noticing that the people who crossed my path weren't random.
The conversations weren't accidental.
The moments of connection weren't coincidences.

Everywhere I went, people found me — or rather, they were sent to me.

Not because I was special.
Not because I had all the answers.
But because I had something rare:

Alignment.
Clarity.
Presence.
Truth.

When you become aligned, you become a lighthouse — not because you try to shine, but because you simply do. Your presence becomes guidance. Your energy becomes direction. Your strength becomes permission for others to rise into theirs.

And I began to understand:

God doesn't save you just to spare your life.
He saves you to use your life.

I survived the crash not just to continue breathing, but to step into something bigger than myself. Something meaningful. Something sacred.

Leadership isn't about having control or authority.
It's about holding light.

The kind of light that helps others see their own path.
The kind of light that reminds people they're not alone.
The kind of light that turns fear into understanding.
The kind of light that turns confusion into clarity.

I wasn't leading with my voice — I was leading with my energy.

People started coming to me with honesty they didn't share with anyone else. They trusted me with their truth, their wounds, their questions, their fears. They had no idea why they felt safe with me — they just did.

And that's when I finally understood something that had been forming inside me since the moment the car crashed:

Purpose doesn't ask for permission.
It reveals itself through responsibility.

I felt responsible for what I had learned.
Responsible for what I had been given.
Responsible for the gift of understanding souls.
Responsible for the peace that now lived in me.
Responsible for the safety people felt in my presence.

Not in a heavy way — in a rightful way.

Purpose is not a burden when it belongs to you.
It is a memory.

Remembering that the version of you who walked out of the wreckage was created for more than survival.
Remembering that your wisdom came from experiences others may never understand.
Remember that your story carries medicine — not just for yourself, but for those who will one day hear it.

I realized that leadership doesn't always look like taking charge.
Sometimes it looks like listening when no one else will.
Sometimes it looks like speaking the truth gently.
Sometimes it looks like being still when the world is loud.
Sometimes it looks like guiding without claiming to guide.

Your calling becomes loud when other people start awakening through your presence — and you don't even notice you're doing it.

People told me I made them feel understood.
That being around me brought them peace.
That my energy felt grounding, comforting, real.
That my perspective shifted something inside them.
That I said things they needed to hear without knowing they needed to hear them.

And none of it was forced.
None of it was planned.
None of it was intentional.

It was simply who I had become.

A guide.
A mirror.
A grounding force.
A spark for awakening in others.

I was saved to lead — not by standing above people, but by standing with them.
By walking ahead when I needed to, beside them when they struggled, and behind them when they found their own strength.

Leadership, I learned, is not about being followed.
It's about being trusted.

And life has given me trust — not through perfection, but through authenticity.

Every wound I healed became wisdom.
Every moment of clarity became a message.
Every spiritual shift became direction.
Every experience became a lesson someone else would one day need.

And standing in that truth, I finally accepted it:

I was not just reborn.
I was commissioned.

My survival was not an accident.
My awakening was not random.
My clarity was not coincidental.

I was saved because there is a path only I can walk.
People only I can reach.
Light only I can hold.

You don't choose a calling.
A calling chooses you.

And mine had chosen me with the force of impact, the silence of surrender, and the clarity of rebirth.

I had been saved for a reason.

And now, I was ready to lead.

CHAPTER 18 — The Weight You No Longer Carry

As I moved deeper into my awakening, I realized something both liberating and devastating:

Most of the weight I had carried my entire life…
was never mine.

Not the expectations.
Not the fears.
Not the doubts.
Not the insecurities whispered into me by others.
Not the pressure to be the strong one, the understanding one, the calm one, the healer, the one who knows what to do.

None of that belonged to me.

I had been carrying the emotional luggage of other people for so long that I mistook it for my own. Their trauma. Their disappointment. Their projections. Their judgment. Their guilt. Their internal battles. Their demons. The ones they didn't want to face, didn't know how to face, or refused to face.

And because I could see souls so clearly — even when I didn't understand what I was doing — I absorbed those energies without recognizing the cost.

I carried burdens that didn't have my name on them.
I held tension that didn't originate from my spirit.
I walked through life weighted down by emotional debris that wasn't mine to clean up.

But awakening brings light to the shadows you didn't know were dimming you.

The more aligned I became, the more I began to understand the difference between:

Your emotions and someone else's energy.
Your intuition and someone else's fear.
Your truth and someone else's expectations.
Your responsibility and someone else's avoidance.

There is a spiritual violence in carrying weight that does not belong to you.
It quietly crushes your potential.
It distorts your identity.
It blinds you to your calling.
It makes you think you are breaking under the weight of your own life, when in reality — you're breaking under the weight of someone else's.

Awakening lifted that illusion.

Suddenly, I could see the threads clearly — who I had been holding, who I had been protecting, who I had been shielding, who I had been emotionally carrying like a backpack strapped across my shoulders for years.

It was never meant to be mine.

And the moment I accepted that, I felt something I had never felt before:

Lightness.

Not physical lightness — spiritual weightlessness.
A freedom in my chest.
A quiet in my mind.
A settling in my bones.
A return to myself.

It was then that truth came to light:

When you stop carrying what isn't yours, your purpose has space to breathe.

My clarity sharpened.
My connection to God deepened.
My intuition strengthened.
My energy rose.
My path became visible.
My calling became undeniable.

Because the noise of other people's weight had been drowning the voice of my own soul.

The crash didn't free me.
Awakening freed me.
Awareness freed me.
Truth freed me.

I learned:

You can love people deeply without holding on to their suffering.
You can support people without sacrificing yourself.
You can guide people without absorbing their pain.
You can care without carrying.

Love is not measured by how much weight you take on — it is measured by how much truth you stand in.

And the truth is:

My purpose requires clarity.
My intuition requires openness.
My spirit requires freedom.
My calling requires lightness.

I couldn't rise while dragging chains that weren't mine.
I couldn't hear God while drowning in noise that didn't originate

from me.

I couldn't step into my aligned self while living through the emotional shadows of others.

So I began releasing.

Releasing the unspoken expectations.
The invisible responsibilities.
The old wounds that weren't mine.
The guilt that wasn't mine.
The pressure that wasn't mine.
The emotional labor no one asked me to do, but everyone silently expected.

And with each release, I felt myself returning.

Not returning to who I used to be —
returning to who I was always meant to be.

Lighter.
Clearer.
More grounded.
More intentional.
More aligned.

I realized something that would redefine the rest of my life;

Your spirit becomes unstoppable the moment you learn what weight is yours and what isn't.

This truth didn't make me cold.
It made me wise.
It made me love in a healthier way.
It made me compassionate without self-destruction.
It made me a leader, not a container for emotional chaos.

Awakening showed me that I was never meant to be a vessel
for other people's unresolved storms —
I was meant to be a lighthouse.

A guide.
A presence.
A reminder of truth.

And a lighthouse does not jump into the ocean to save ships; it
shines so they can find their own way.

This chapter of my life marked the first moment I stood fully
in that role.

I was no longer drowning in weight that wasn't mine.
I was standing —
clear, steady, aligned.

Ready for the next step of my purpose.

CHAPTER 19 — The Lessons You Don't Learn Until You Live Them

There are lessons we hear about our whole lives — lessons people repeat to us, lessons written in books, lessons wrapped in quotes and advice.
But some lessons can't be understood through words.

Some lessons must be lived.

They must break you open.
They must quiet your world.
They must shake everything you thought you knew.
They must be experienced in a way no explanation could ever replicate.

After the crash, after stepping into alignment, I began to see how many truths had been sitting in front of me my entire life — truths I wasn't ready to understand until I lived them.

One of the first lessons was this:

1. You grow through what you survive.

Not around it. Not in spite of it. Through it.

People love to talk about healing like it's pretty — like it's soft, peaceful, and gentle.
But real healing is confrontational.
Real healing demands truth.
Real healing asks you to walk through the fire instead of pretending it doesn't burn.

The crash didn't just force me into clarity —
It forced me into the truth.

Truth about who I was.
Truth about who I wasn't.
Truth about what mattered.
Truth about what didn't.
Truth about the lessons I hadn't wanted to face.

And once I saw the truth, I couldn't unsee it.

2. Not every storm comes to destroy you.

Some come to reveal you.

People assume tragedy is punishment.
But sometimes, it is alignment.

The moment the world stopped spinning inside that car was the moment my spirit finally settled.
Not in fear — in understanding.

Everything I had been ignoring, suppressing, avoiding, or postponing came into perfect clarity.
It was like God said:

"You asked for alignment.
This is the doorway."

I wasn't meant to break.
I was meant to awake.

3. Death teaches you how to live.

When you come face to face with the possibility of not having another breath, something changes inside you that can never return to what it once was.

Your priorities shift.
Your awareness sharpens.

Your gratitude expands.
Your tolerance for bullshit disappears.

Life becomes precious — not in a dramatic way, but in a deeply intentional way.

The small things become sacred.
The quiet moments become healing.
The people who love you become treasures.
And every sunrise becomes a reason.

4. Peace is a choice, not a condition.

I used to think peace came from things being stable — from life being predictable, smooth, calm, easy.
But peace is internal.
Peace is discipline.
Peace is choosing alignment over chaos, every. single. time.

I now protect my peace with the same intensity I once protected other people's feelings.
I guard my energy.
I honor my boundaries.
I choose myself.

Not because I am selfish.
But because I finally understand the cost of abandoning myself.

5. The universe removes what you won't walk away from.

People.
Habits.
Thoughts.
Behaviors.
Environments.
Identities.

Anything that is out of alignment will eventually fall away —
gently if you allow it, violently if you resist it.
The crash was the violent removal of everything I refused to let go
of.

And even though it shook me, it also freed me.

6. You cannot become who you are meant to be while staying
who you used to be.

This was the hardest lesson.

Because growth requires shedding.
Shedding requires endings.
Endings require grief.

I had to mourn the versions of myself that survived for so long
without knowing how to live.
I had to release identities built from fear, from conditioning, from
trying to be everything for everyone else.

Becoming my aligned self wasn't an addition —
It was a removal.

Removing weight.
Removing expectations.
Removing outdated beliefs.
Removing the masks I didn't even know I wore.

Only then could I rise.

7. What is meant for you will always find you — but only when
you're awake enough to feel it

Opportunities.
People.
Healing.
Purpose.

Abundance.
Love.

These things weren't waiting for the "perfect moment."
They were waiting for the aligned version of me —
the version who wasn't drowning in unnecessary weight,
the version who trusted her intuition,
the version who rose on purpose instead of fear.

And once I became that version, life began to meet me in
places it never could before.

8. You don't truly understand life until life almost leaves you.

This is the lesson no one wants but everyone needs.

Facing death stripped away everything false.
Everything is temporary.
Everything that never mattered.

It left me with the bare truth of my existence:

I was alive.
I was meant to be here.
I had a purpose.
And I would never again live my life half-awake.

These lessons didn't arrive gently.
They arrived through impact, silence, surrender, awakening.

But they arrived exactly when they needed to.

And once I lived them — not read them, not heard them, not
imagined them — once I lived them, everything in my life shifted.

Because true lessons don't change your mind.
They change your soul.

CHAPTER 20 — The Rise of the New Identity

Becoming your aligned self isn't a moment — it's a claiming.

A claim of your truth.
A claim of your purpose.
A claim of every piece of you that survived the fire, the breaking, the confusion, the crash, the awakening.

This chapter of my life wasn't just about growing.
It was about stepping into a new identity with intention —
with clarity, with confidence, with a presence that no longer apologized for existing.

The old me would have tried to ease the transition.
Would have tried to soften herself so people wouldn't notice the change.
Would have tried to explain why she was becoming different.
Would have tried to hold on to relationships that could not grow with her.

But awakening doesn't allow you to return to smallness.

Once you know who you are, you cannot go back to pretending you don't.

The new identity rising within me came with a few undeniable truths:

I was no longer someone who hid her intuition.

I used to question myself.
Now I trusted myself.
My intuition wasn't a feeling — it was guidance.
It wasn't random — it was spiritual intelligence.

I stopped asking, "Is this real?"
And started saying, "This is the truth."

I no longer apologized for my presence.

The old me walked into rooms wondering if she belonged.
The new me walked in understanding that belonging is internal —
never external.

I didn't shrink.
I didn't over-explain.
I didn't dim my light to make others comfortable.

I stood as myself, fully, completely, unapologetically.

I no longer took responsibility for others' emotions.

For years I carried people — their pain, their problems, their
projections.
But aligned identity requires boundaries.

I learned:

I can care without carrying.
I can support without absorbing.
I can love without sacrificing myself.

Compassion remained — but codependency dissolved.

I honored my voice.

For so long, I swallowed my truth.
I softened my edges.
I protected other people's comfort over my own clarity.

But now my voice held weight — not because I spoke louder,
but because I spoke from truth.
From understanding.
From a place where fear no longer silenced me.

My words became extensions of my soul.

Walk with purpose — not haste.

The old me rushed through life trying to keep up.
The new me moved intentionally, with awareness and presence.

I didn't react; I responded.
I didn't chase; I magnetized.
I didn't force; I allowed.
I didn't grasp; I trusted.

Life moved with me because I moved with purpose.

Embrace solitude, not as loneliness, but as alignment.

Silence became healing.
Time alone became clarity.
Stillness became sacred.

I no longer rushed to fill empty moments with noise or people.
My spirit was no longer afraid of itself.

Solitude became the place where my identity sharpened the most.

I recognized my calling — fully, finally, and without hesitation.

This new identity didn't wander or question like the old one.
She understood her place.
She understood her purpose.
She understood why she survived.

The leader in me emerged.
The healer in me strengthened.
The intuitive in me expanded.
The vessel in me opened.

I was not just living — I was embodying.

As this new identity rose within me, I felt something I had never experienced before:

Wholeness.

Not perfection.
Not control.
Not certainty.

Wholeness.

A complete acceptance of myself —
my past, my pain, my gifts, my spirit, my purpose.

The pieces of me that once felt scattered finally fit together. Not because life became easy, but because I became aligned.

The world didn't change —
I did.

And the more I embraced this identity, the more life responded.

Doors opened.
Opportunities aligned.
People appeared.
Lessons made sense.
Purpose expanded.

Because life always meets you at the level of your identity.

And now, I was walking in the identity of a woman who understood:

I survived for a reason.
I woke up for a reason.
I am here for a reason.

My new identity wasn't an upgrade.
It was a rebirth.

And I was finally ready to live from that place —
fully, without looking back.

CHAPTER 21 — Alignment as a Daily Practice

Awakening is a moment.
Alignment is a discipline.

It's easy to feel clear during the breakthrough, during the transformation, during the miracle that wakes you up.
But the real work — the real becoming — happens in the days that follow.
In the quiet.
In the routines.
In the choices that seem small but define everything.

After stepping into my new identity, I realized something:
Staying aligned isn't automatic.
It's intentional.
It's active.
It's alive.

Alignment is not a destination you reach.
It is a way of walking.

A way of thinking.
A way of responding.
A way of protecting your energy.
A way of honoring your intuition every single day.

This chapter of my life became about practice — the consistent steps that kept me connected to myself, to God, to purpose, to peace.

I stopped letting every emotion pull me into chaos.
I stopped feeding situations that didn't match my energy.
I stopped rushing to respond just to silence or prove a point.

Peace became my default, not my reward.

And when something attempted to pull me out of alignment, I asked:

Is this mine to hold? Is this worth my energy? Does this align with who I am becoming?

If the answer was no, I let it fall away.

Instead of living in my head, I lived in the moment.

I breathed slower.
I noticed more.
I moved with intention.

Presence grounded me in ways I never knew I needed — because you can't walk on purpose if your mind is everywhere except here.

No more second-guessing.
No more doubting myself.
No more trying to rationalize what my spirit already knew.

Alignment feels like ease.
Misalignment feels like tension.

It became simple:

Not everything needed my hands on it.
Not every situation needed my intervention.
Not every emotion needed to be fixed.

I learned to trust the unfolding.
To trust timing.
To trust the path I was guided toward.
To trust that what was meant for me would arrive without force.

Releasing control didn't make me powerless.
It made me competent.

I stopped saying yes to things that drained me.
I stopped shrinking for people who didn't rise with me.
I stopped explaining myself to those committed to misunderstanding me.

My boundaries became an act of self-love —
not walls, but filters.

A way of saying:

Only what nurtures my spirit can stay.

Not just for the big things, but the small ones:

A peaceful morning.
A deep conversation.
A moment of clarity.
A breath that felt easy.
A day without heaviness.
The simple fact that I was alive.

Gratitude sharpened my awareness of the blessings I once overlooked.
It raised my frequency.
It aligned me even deeper.

Whether it was guiding someone, speaking truth, listening without judgment, or simply being present —
I lived my purpose in small, everyday actions.

Leadership wasn't something I did.
It was something I embodied.

And the more I honored it, the louder my calling became.
It felt like evolution.

A natural part of becoming.

As these practices settled into my daily life, I began to feel something shift inside me:

Consistency became transformation.
Intention became intuition.
Awareness became wisdom.
Alignment became my lifestyle — not my event.

This was no longer about the crash.
No longer about the awakening.
No longer about the moment everything changed.

This was about who I was choosing to be every day.

And I realized:

Awakening is the spark.
Alignment is the flame.
The purpose is the fire.

To stay aligned meant living with discipline, clarity, and reverence for the life I was given.

My days felt different.
My choices felt cleaner.
My spirit felt lighter.
My path felt clearer.

Alignment became my rhythm.

Not perfection.
Not control.
Just truth — lived daily.

And with each day, my identity rooted itself deeper into purpose, shaping the next evolution of who I was becoming.

This was no longer a journey of survival.
It was a journey of mastery.

CHAPTER 22 — When Life Begins to Mirror Your Alignment

There is a moment — quiet, subtle, almost unnoticeable at first — when the world around you begins to shift in response to who you are becoming.

Not because life suddenly becomes easier.
Not because everything falls perfectly into place.
But because you have changed, and life has no choice but to change with you.

As I continued to walk in alignment, I started to see my surroundings reflect that alignment back to me. It wasn't magic. It wasn't a coincidence. It was resonance — life matching the frequency of the person I had grown into.

The first changes were internal.
The next changes were external.
And the deepest changes were spiritual.

Opportunities began to flow with ease.

I wasn't chasing things anymore.
I wasn't forcing answers.
I wasn't trying to make life bend to my will.

Instead, opportunities found me.

Paths I never considered opened.
People who aligned with my purpose appeared.
Moments that felt divinely timed unfolded effortlessly.

It felt like life was saying:

"Now that you're aligned, I can finally send you what you were always meant to have."

The wrong people drifted away — effortlessly.

There was no argument.
No explosion.
No drama.
Just distance.

Distance created by growth.
By clarity.
By my new energy refusing to entertain what I once tolerated.

People who thrived off chaos no longer felt drawn to me.
People who needed my old self no longer recognized me.
People who took without giving lost access to me.

It wasn't rejection —
It resonated.

They no longer matched the frequency of my spirit.

The right people felt magnetic.

Conversations deepened.
Connections strengthened.
Relationships felt intentional instead of draining.

The people who aligned with the new version of me brought peace, inspiration, depth, and reciprocity.
They matched my growth.
They respected my boundaries.
They honored my spirit.

They didn't just take space —
they held space.

My intuition became impossibly clear.

There was no more guessing.
No more doubting.
No more questioning whether something was "just in my head."

When something wasn't aligned, my spirit reacted instantly.
When something was aligned, it felt like a full-body yes.

I had finally learned the difference between fear and intuition
—
one restricts you, the other guides you.

Stress didn't hit me the same way.
Obstacles didn't shake me.
People's opinions didn't influence my path.
Moments of uncertainty no longer scared me.

My foundation was internal now, not external.

I no longer leaned on circumstances to feel grounded.
I leaned on alignment.
In spirit.
In truth.

Repeating numbers.
Meaningful coincidences.
Messages through people.
Dreams that felt like guidance.
Signs that felt placed directly in my path.

These weren't random —
They were confirmations.

They were reminders that I was exactly where I was meant to
be.

The universe speaks loudly when you've finally learned how to listen.

I didn't need a detailed plan.
I didn't need certainty.
I didn't need control.

I trusted the pull.
I trusted the alignment.
I trusted myself.

My purpose became clearer through experience, through intuition, through the way life responded to my energy.

I realized:

Alignment is not about having all the answers —
It's about trusting the path even when you can't see the entire map.

I sat with peace. Not casually. But with the state of it becoming lived naturally.

Like every second that passed was an extra day I walked.

Peace was not a state I fought for.
Not a state I begged for.
A state I lived in.

Peace wasn't the absence of challenges —
it was the presence of clarity.

I understood what deserved my reaction and what didn't.
I recognized the difference between temporary discomfort and true misalignment.
I honored my boundaries without guilt.

Peace wasn't something I protected —
it was something I embodied.

As life mirrored my alignment, I understood something life-changing:

You do not create a better life by controlling it.
You create a better life by becoming someone awake enough to receive it.

Everything I lost made room for what was meant for me.
Everything that left created space for everything that was coming.
Everything that felt uncertain became proof of trust.

My world wasn't changing because I was lucky.
My world was changing because I had changed.

Once you rise into alignment, the universe rises to meet you.

The external world reflects the internal one.
Your energy becomes your compass.
Your purpose becomes your path.
Your alignment becomes your magnet.

And life —
beautifully, intentionally, divinely —
begins to respond.

CHAPTER 23 — Walking With Purpose

There comes a point in every transformation where the inner work begins to move outward.
Where alignment stops being something you feel inside your spirit
—
and becomes something you live in your steps, your choices, your presence, your voice.

For a long time, my awakening was internal.
Quiet.
Personal.
Sacred.

But purpose isn't meant to stay inside you.
Purpose is meant to move.

It's meant to stretch into the world and become something others can feel, witness, and grow from.
And it was then that I realized:

I was no longer just someone who survived a miracle.
I was someone meant to walk in that miracle.

Not talk about it.
Not hide it.
Not shrink away from it.
Walk in it.

Intentionally.
Boldly.
Spiritually.
Continuously.

As my alignment deepened, I began to notice a shift in the way I carried myself — not in how I looked, but in how I moved through the world.

I no longer drifted.
I no longer lived on autopilot.
I no longer rushed through moments without noticing them.

Every day had purpose woven into it.
Every interaction held potential.
Every breath felt sacred.

The world around me hadn't changed —
but I had become someone who walked through it differently.

Before, I moved toward things because they were familiar, expected, convenient, or available.
Now, I moved toward what was aligned.
If it didn't feel like the truth, I didn't go.
If it didn't honor my spirit, I stepped back.
If it didn't contribute to my purpose, I released it.

I began choosing paths with clarity instead of fear.

I started showing up fully.

Not halfway.
Not quietly.
Not hiding the depth of who I was.

Whether I was talking to a friend, helping a stranger, walking into a room, or simply existing —
I showed up with a presence.

People felt that.
People responded to that.
People trusted that.

Because authenticity is magnetic.
And aligned authenticity is transformative.

I didn't have to convince anyone of my growth.
I didn't have to prove that I had changed.
I didn't have to justify why my energy was different.

My life itself became evidence.
My peace became my explanation.
My boundaries became my clarity.
My alignment became my language.

People understood my transformation without needing the story behind it.

I began to carry myself like someone who had just woken up for the first time.

Every sunrise felt intentional.
Every breath felt borrowed.
Every moment felt like something God had chosen for me.

Not in a dramatic way —
in a grounded way.

The kind of groundedness that only comes after brushing against the edge of death and choosing to live differently.

There were decisions I made that made no sense to anyone else.
There were shifts that didn't follow a plan.
There were moves I made because my intuition said "now," not because I had figured out every detail.

Purpose rarely asks for a plan.
It asks for trust.

And I began trusting with a certainty that surprised even me.

People came to me with questions.
With emotions.
With their truths.
Not because I positioned myself as a healer, but because my
alignment created space for them to understand themselves.

Guidance wasn't something I forced —
it became something I naturally embodied.

And that is when I realized:

Walking with purpose doesn't mean you always know where
you're going.
It means you trust the steps you take.

The more aligned I became, the more life aligned with me.
Blessings flowed without force.
Connections deepened without effort.
Opportunities appeared without searching.
Clarity arrived without struggle.

Purpose moves toward you the moment you walk toward
yourself.

As I continued walking in purpose, I understood something
deeper than anything I'd learned before:

Your life becomes your calling the moment your actions match
your disipline.

Not your words.
Not your hopes.
Not your dreams.

Your actions.

Purpose isn't what you feel —
it's what you do with what you feel.

It's how you lead when no one is watching.
It's how you love when no one is giving you credit.
It's how you show up when no one asks you to.
It's how you continue walking even when the path isn't clear.

In this life, purpose became my compass.
My steps became my message.
My life became my leadership.

I was no longer simply aligned —
I was walking in alignment.

With intention.
With clarity.
With courage.

And with a deep, unshakeable knowing:

I was moving in the direction God created me for.

CHAPTER 24 — The Responsibility of Awakening

Awakening is not a reward.
It is a responsibility.

Most people think spiritual awakening is about feeling enlightened, peaceful, or special.
But in reality, awakening places a weight on your shoulders — not a heavy weight, but a sacred one.

A weight that says:

"Now that you see the truth, you can't pretend you don't."
"Now that you understand the world differently, you must move differently."
"Now that you have clarity, you are responsible for how you use it."

This was the chapter where I finally understood that my journey wasn't just personal.
It was purposeful.

Everything I had survived…
everything I had learned…
everything I had awakened to…

was meant to be used.

Not hoarded.
Not hidden.
Not kept within the walls of my own mind.

My awakening was not only mine —
it was meant to be shared.

Not in a performative way.
Not in a way that demanded recognition.
But in a way that allowed others to rise through the light I carried.

And with that revelation came the deeper truth:

Clarity comes with responsibility.

I had been given insight that many people spend their whole
lives searching for —
insight into the soul, into purpose, into alignment, into healing, into
energy.

And once you understand something deeply...
once you've lived through transformation...
once you've walked through fire and come out still glowing...

you are responsible for how you exist in the world afterward.

Not to fix people.
Not to save them.
Not to carry their weight.

But to embody what you've learned.

To walk with integrity.
To move with compassion.
To speak with intention.
To listen with presence.
To guide without ego.
To stand in truth even when it would be easier to shrink.

Awakening asks you to lead by example.

Not by force.
Not by claiming authority.
Not by trying to be above anyone else.

But by being aligned —
so deeply aligned that your presence alone shifts the atmosphere.

Some people think leadership is about telling others what to do.
But real leadership — spiritual leadership — looks like this:

• You rise, and others feel permission to rise too.
• You heal, and others feel safe enough to heal.
• You speak the truth, and others find courage to speak theirs.
• You stand in alignment, and others learn what alignment looks like.

Leadership is not something you announce.
It is something you become.

Awakening also reveals who cannot go with you.

And that's part of the responsibility.

You cannot stay small for people who are committed to misunderstanding your growth.
You cannot dim your intuition because someone else fears their own truth.
You cannot return to old environments where your spirit suffocated just to make others comfortable.

Responsibility means choosing your path even when it separates you from familiar faces.

Not out of arrogance —
out of alignment.

Your energy becomes your influence.

People watch how you move before they listen to what you say.
They observe how you respond to conflict, to stress, to uncertainty.

They notice the peace you carry, the boundaries you keep, the clarity you speak with.

You become a mirror that reflects what's possible.

And with that influence comes responsibility —
to stay true, to stay aligned, to stay grounded in who you have become.

Awakening requires discipline.

Discipline with your thoughts.
Discipline with your emotions.
Discipline with your choices.
Discipline with your reactions.

Because once you are aware, you cannot act unaware again without feeling it break something inside you.

Your spirit knows better now.
Your intuition is louder.
Your alignment is sharper.
Your boundaries are clearer.

Awakening doesn't make life easier —
It makes you stronger.

Stronger in truth.
Stronger in self-control.
Stronger in compassion.
Stronger in purpose.

Awakening turns your life into a message.

Not a sermon.
Not a performance.
Not a story you force on others.

A message written on how you treat people.
How you handle challenges.
How you honor yourself.
How you walk through the world.

Some will understand it.
Some won't.
But the message still matters.

Because someone out there is watching you and learning how to save themselves.

CHAPTER 25 — The Expansion of the Self

There comes a point in your journey where healing is no longer the focus —
becoming is.

Up until now, so much of my path had revolved around recovering, releasing, understanding, shedding, awakening, and aligning. It was a deep internal homecoming, a rebuilding of my foundation, a reconnection with my spirit after years of carrying weight that never belonged to me.

But healing is not the final destination.
Healing is preparation.

And once the healing settled into my bones — once the noise quieted, the confusion dissolved, and my purpose became louder than my fear — something new began to rise:

Expansion.

Expansion feels different from healing.
Healing is inward.
Expansion is outward.
Healing asks you to look within.
Expansion asks you to step forward.

It was in this chapter of my life that I began to feel myself stretching — spiritually, emotionally, intuitively, energetically.
Not painfully.
Not forcefully.
Naturally.

Like I had finally grown roots, and now it was time to grow branches.

For years, I thought of myself based on what I had survived, what I had overcome, what had broken me, what I'd endured. But expansion required me to shift my identity:

I was no longer the girl who was healing.
I was the woman who was rising.

My life was no longer defined by what hurt me.
It was defined by what awakened me.

Expansion demanded that I step into spaces I once felt unworthy of.

Leadership roles.
New opportunities.
Spiritual callings.
Deeper connections.
Higher standards.
Bolder dreams.

Not because I suddenly felt "ready,"
but because alignment had prepared me even when I didn't realize it.

I walked into rooms differently.
I existed differently.
My energy arrived before I did.

And life responded.

The old me only felt safe with what was predictable.
The aligned me understood that purpose thrives in the unknown.

I didn't have every detail figured out —
and I didn't need to.

I followed the pull.
I trusted the whisper.
I stepped where I was guided, not where I was certain.

And every time I trusted, something in me grew.

My intuition sharpened.
My ability to read energy deepened.
My compassion became a form of wisdom.
My presence became healing for others.
My words carried weight.
My insight carried the truth.

These weren't traits — They were tools.

Tools for purpose.
Tools for leadership.
Tools for guiding others into alignment.

Expansion meant recognizing these gifts not as coincidences,
but as assignments.

Silence became my teacher.
Stillness became my anchor.
Reflection became my superpower.

Instead of fearing being alone with my thoughts,
I craved it —
because that was where my spirit expanded the most.

In solitude, I heard myself clearly.
I heard God clearly.
I heard my intuition clearly.

The world gets loud.
Alignment speaks in quiet.

I no longer felt behind. I no longer felt rushed.
I no longer felt like I needed to meet invisible deadlines.

Expansion taught me that everything arrives at the moment it
is meant to.
Not sooner.
Not later.

The timing of my awakening was perfect.
The timing of my rebirth was perfect.
The timing of my expansion was perfect.

Life wasn't delaying anything —
It was preparing everything.

Expansion brought a deeper sense of purpose.

Purpose wasn't a question anymore.
It wasn't a possibility.
It wasn't a distant dream.

It was the truth.

A truth that lived inside me.
A truth that moved through me.
A truth that expanded every time I listened to it.

Purpose didn't demand that I change the world.
Purpose demanded that I change my world —
and let the ripple extend naturally.

Expansion felt like stepping into a version of myself I had
been destined to meet.
A version who stood taller.
Loved deeper.
Spoke truer.
Understood more.
Trusted fully.

Moved with intention.
Listened to her spirit above all else.

This wasn't confidence.
This wasn't ego.
This wasn't a performance.

This was destiny unfolding.

I was expanding into the woman I was always meant to
become —
the woman who survived the crash,
heard the call,
answered the call,
and now walked boldly into purpose without slowing herself down.

Expansion wasn't just about becoming more.
It was about becoming who I truly am.

And as I stepped into its presence,
I understood:

Healing awakened me.
Alignment grounded me.
But expansion…
expansion prepared me to step into the life that had been waiting
for me.

CHAPTER 26 — Stepping Into the Higher Calling

Expansion wasn't the end of my transformation —
It was the doorway to something even bigger, something deeper,
something sacred.

As I grew into the aligned version of myself, as my awareness
sharpened and my purpose became clearer, I realized I was
standing on the edge of something I couldn't yet name.
It wasn't fear.
It wasn't uncertainty.
It was destiny.

A higher calling.

A calling I had felt in pieces throughout my life —
in the way strangers confided in me,
in the way I could read emotions without words,
in the way my presence seemed to soothe or awaken something in
others,
In this way I attracted people seeking clarity, truth, grounding.

But now, after everything I had lived through,
that calling was no longer whispering.

It was speaking.
Loudly.
Directly.
Undeniably.

There was no permission to seek, no validation to collect, no
preparation checklist to follow.

The calling rose inside me like something ancient, familiar, and meant —
a pull that came from a place deeper than desire.

I was ready,not, because I had perfected myself,
but because I had aligned myself.

Awakening prepares you.
Expansion positions you.
Purpose calls you.

And when purpose calls, it does not negotiate.

For so long, I second-guessed the parts of myself that set me apart:

My intuition.
My insight.
My emotional intelligence.
My ability to feel people deeply.
My ability to see through lies, masks, and illusions.
My ability to guide without trying.
My ability to sense the spiritual even when no one said a word.

These weren't accidents.
These weren't quirks.
These weren't coincidences.

These were tools —
tools I was being asked to use with intention.

The higher calling didn't just ask me to accept my gifts.
It asked me to embody them.
To trust them.
To lead with them.

The purpose wasn't about a title.
It wasn't about a job.
It wasn't about impressing anyone.

Purpose was influence —
the influence of presence,
of clarity,
of alignment.

Purpose was impact —
not explosive,
but subtle,
quiet,
consistent,
transformative.

Purpose was guidance —
not as a savior,
but as an example.

Purpose was service —
not the draining kind,
but the kind that pours from overflow.

Purpose was spiritual —
not religious,
not performative,
but energetic, intuitive, destined.

I understood now that my life was not random. My survival
was not random. My awakening was not random.

I was being prepared.

Prepared to guide.
Prepared to teach.
Prepared to influence.

Prepared to hold space for others.
Prepared to walk a path that few are brave enough to step onto.

Not because they are incapable —
but because awakening demands courage.

Courage to be different.
Courage to be honest.
Courage to be aligned in a world that benefits from your confusion.

But I no longer feared standing out.
I feared shrinking back into a version of myself that no longer existed.

The people I was meant to reach were in the spotlight continuously.

Not everyone — just the ones who felt my frequency.

The ones who were searching.
The ones who were hurting.
The ones who were awakening.
The ones who needed grounding.
The ones who needed someone who could see their soul without judgment.

I didn't chase these people.
They appeared.
And I recognized them instantly —
not by their words, but by the resonance.

They were drawn to my clarity.
To my peace.
To my courage.
To my story.
To the way I walked through the world after dying and waking up different.

My calling was not to change the whole world —
but to change the worlds of the people meant to cross my path.

The calling revealed a truth I could no longer deny:

I had not just rebuilt myself.
I had evolved.

Into a guide.
Into a leader.
Into a healer.
Into a mirror.
Into a vessel.

Not by choice —
by chance.

I had become someone who could walk into a room and shift
the energy without saying a word.
Someone whose presence alone spoke truth.
Someone whose life itself was a message.

The calling asked me to rise — fully.

Not halfway.
Not cautiously.
Not timidly.

But boldly.

Into purpose.
Into leadership.
Into influence.
Into spiritual maturity.
Into the woman God designed me to be.

No more shrinking. No more doubting. No more hesitating.

This was the moment where my transformation moved into a mission.

Where everything I had learned became everything I was meant to give.
Where everything I had survived became everything I would one day teach.
Where everything I had awakened to become the foundation of the life I was building next.

This wasn't just a calling.

It was a commission.

A divine assignment.

A higher purpose unfolding through every breath I took.

And as I stepped into it — fully, knowingly, powerfully — I understood:

My life wasn't just saved.
It was claimed.
For something greater.
For something bigger.
For something holy.

CHAPTER 27 — The Energy You Carry Into the World

Your peace speaks long before your words do.
So do your boundaries, your truth, your alignment. Energy communicates what language never fully can.

I began to understand that my presence was no longer neutral. It carried weight. It carried clarity. It carried a frequency that moved through spaces without effort or intention. I didn't have to explain myself. I didn't have to assert authority. The authority lived within me.

When I entered the room, something shifted. Not because I demanded attention, but because alignment commands its own gravity. Conversations deepened. Superficiality dissolved. People softened, reflected, and opened. I wasn't trying to influence anything — influence happened because coherence is powerful.

A calm presence disarms chaos.
A grounded spirit steadies uprooted hearts.
A clear mind helps others see themselves honestly.
A healed person awakens healing in those who are ready.

This became my new reality. I wasn't just walking in alignment — I was walking in impact.

And with that realization came responsibility.

Purpose, I learned, isn't revealed only through action. It is revealed through presence. People may forget your words. They may forget what you did. But they will never forget how your energy made them feel.

My calling was never only to heal myself.
It was to exist in a way that made healing possible for others.

My energy became a gift.
A compass.
A responsibility.
A light.

And I committed to carrying it into the world with intention.

CHAPTER 28 — The Loneliness of Transformation

People celebrate your awakening. They applaud your clarity, your rebirth, your growth. But few talk about what comes after — the quiet, disorienting loneliness that follows transformation.

Not the loneliness of being alone.
Not the absence of people.
But the loneliness of no longer belonging where you once fit.

It arrives subtly, as your perspective shifts and your energy elevates. As your boundaries strengthen, your intuition sharpens, and your calling grows louder, something else happens — your world begins to thin out. Not because you are better than anyone, but because alignment changes your frequency.

You no longer tolerate shallow connections. You no longer entertain chaos disguised as familiarity. You no longer bend for comfort or accept half-presence, half-love, half-truths. The versions of yourself that were once necessary quietly expire — and with them, the relationships that relied on those versions.

People drift. Some step back. Others disappear entirely. Not because you pushed them away, but because your spirit no longer vibrates where it used to.

Loneliness, I learned, is not a punishment.
It is a transition.

In the silence, I met myself without distraction. I learned what I truly valued, what my heart genuinely needed, and what depth actually felt like. I stopped wanting to be surrounded and started wanting to be understood.

That shift narrowed my circle — but strengthened my soul.

I also realized something difficult but freeing: not everyone can meet you at the level you've reached. Some people only know how to relate to the version of you that lacked boundaries, that stayed quiet to keep peace, that gave endlessly without protection. When you evolve beyond those dynamics, it can feel like loss to them — but for you, it is liberation.

Loneliness became my teacher. It taught me how to be my own companion. How to sit with my thoughts, regulate my emotions, trust my inner voice, and comfort myself without reaching outward for validation.

And slowly, I understood — I was never truly alone. I simply needed space to hear myself clearly.

The loneliness didn't last forever. It was a sacred pause. A clearing. A preparation. And in that space, the universe quietly arranged new connections — ones aligned with who I was becoming, not who I had been.

People who felt like home, not lessons.
People who walked beside me, not behind me.
People who saw me, not just needed me.

Loneliness became proof of transformation. Confirmation that I was growing, evolving, rising. You cannot bring everyone to the place your spirit is heading — and that is not failure. It is alignment.

By the time the connection returned, I had grown roots so deep that nothing could shake me again. Because once you learn how to stand with yourself, loneliness no longer breaks you.

It builds you.

CHAPTER 29 — Guided by Something Greater

There comes a moment in every awakening when you realize you are no longer walking alone. Not emotionally. Not socially. Spiritually.

You begin to sense a quiet orchestration beneath your life — moments lining up too precisely, people appearing at exactly the right time, doors closing with purpose, paths opening without force. What once felt like coincidence begins to feel intentional.

This was the chapter where I understood I was being guided.

Not by chance.
Not by randomness.
But by something wiser than logic and deeper than fear.

Before the crash, I ignored guidance. I called it overthinking. I dismissed intuition. I rationalized discomfort. But after awakening, I recognized those sensations for what they were — messages, protection, direction.

Guidance doesn't arrive loudly. It begins as a nudge. A pull. A quiet knowing. A subtle discomfort that says not this, or go there, or pay attention. And the moment I stopped resisting those signals, clarity flowed.

The "random" moments weren't random.
The delays were protection.
The endings were redirected.
The losses were clearing.

I began to see protection retroactively — how I had been saved from people, choices, and environments that would have derailed my spirit. Rejection revealed itself as mercy. Detours as divine design.

Guidance also came through people. Through strangers, conversations, and departures that made space I didn't yet understand. Every encounter carried meaning — a mirror, a lesson, or an alignment.

The more aligned I became, the clearer the guidance grew. Not louder — but steadier. My intuition stopped whispering. It spoke. My path stopped confusing me. It unfolded.

And then I realized something profound: guidance was never external.

It lived within me.

It was my higher self — the version of me connected to God, to purpose, to destiny. The part of me that already knew where I was going.

Once I understood that, fear loosened its grip. Because the unknown no longer felt empty. It felt intentional.

I was guided.
Held.
Supported.
And destined.

CHAPTER 30 — Becoming the Architect of Your Reality

There comes a moment in every awakening when you stop living like life is something happening to you, and you begin to recognize the truth: life is responding to you. Not to your performance, not to your image, not even to your words—but to what you carry within you. Your energy. Your intention. Your alignment.

Before, I moved through my days in a reactive state. I reacted to problems, to people, to circumstances, to fear. I lived as if survival was the only goal, as if making it through was enough. But once alignment entered my life, everything shifted. I started noticing how the world seemed to rearrange itself based on the way I showed up. When I walked with clarity, situations became clearer. When I moved with intention, doors opened with intention. When I chose peace, chaos had less access to me. When I honored my worth, the world mirrored it back.

I began to understand something simple, but revolutionary: my inner world was building my external world. Thoughts weren't random. Emotions weren't meaningless. Desires weren't accidental. They were part of the architecture—the unseen structure behind the life I was creating.

The more I accepted that truth, the more intentional I became. I stopped letting my emotions drive the wheel and started asking myself a deeper question: what aligns with my highest self? That question changed the way I chose everything—what I allowed, what I entertained, what I pursued, what I released. It was no longer about what felt easy in the moment. It was about what felt true.

And I learned that manifestation is not force. It's frequency. You don't manifest what you want—you manifest what you are. As I became more aligned, I stopped chasing. I started receiving. The right people appeared. The right opportunities found me. My path began to unfold with less resistance—not because life became perfect, but because I became coherent.

Still, I learned that co-creation requires movement. Faith doesn't mean sitting still and hoping. It means showing up. Taking the step. Choosing courage when the outcome isn't visible yet. Momentum isn't born from perfection. It's born from consistency.

There was responsibility in this, too. Because once you realize you are shaping your reality, you can no longer blame the world for what you keep allowing. You can't crave peace while entertaining chaos. You can't desire abundance while feeding scarcity. You can't ask for purpose while living in patterns that contradict it. Creating your reality demands honesty—the kind that leaves no room for excuses.

And then I understood something even deeper: destiny isn't a straight line. It's a collaboration. You meet destiny through alignment. You shape it through intention. You accelerate it through action. You embody it through discipline.

I wasn't powerless. I wasn't random. I wasn't waiting for my life to begin. I was building it—moment by moment, choice by choice, breath by breath.

CHAPTER 31 — Emotional Mastery and the Power of Inner Stillness

After awakening, after alignment, after stepping into purpose and co-creation, life brought me into a different kind of strength—one that didn't look like survival at all. It looked like emotional mastery.

True emotional mastery isn't suppression. It isn't pretending you don't feel. It isn't "being strong" in a way that denies your humanity. It is awareness. It is learning how to witness your emotions without becoming controlled by them. It is hearing what they're trying to say and responding from wisdom instead of reaction.

Before, my emotions didn't control me through dramatic outbursts. They controlled me through subtle patterns—overthinking, anxiety, emotional exhaustion, absorbing the weight of others. I carried feelings that weren't mine and called it empathy. I lived with stress that didn't belong to me and called it responsibility. I felt everything, but I didn't always understand it.

Then alignment sharpened my awareness. I learned to feel emotions rising inside me before they took over. I learned to recognize what was mine and what wasn't. I learned to separate my feelings from reality. Not every thought is true. Not every emotional reaction is a prophecy. Sometimes an emotion is simply an echo from the past asking to be healed in the present.

Stillness became my anchor. Not silence—presence. The ability to pause. To breathe. To observe without absorbing. To hear intuition above the noise of the mind. When life shook me, stillness held me. When emotions surged, stillness guided me. When someone projected onto me, stillness protected me.

And one of the greatest freedoms I ever gave myself was stopping the habit of personalizing other people's emotions. Their tone, their mood, their distance, their frustration—none of it was a measure of my worth. People act from their level of healing. Their triggers are not my responsibility.

I learned that boundaries were emotional medicine. Filters that protected my energy and preserved my peace. I stopped abandoning myself to soothe other people. I stopped carrying emotional chaos that wasn't mine to hold. I stopped negotiating my stability for someone else's comfort.

Emotional mastery didn't mean I was never triggered. It meant I handled triggers differently. I reflected instead of reacting. I grounded instead of spiraling. I chose consciousness over autopilot.

And as I grew fluent in my own emotional language, I realized: emotions are messengers. Fear, anger, sadness, discomfort—they all have something to teach you. The goal isn't to become numb. The goal is to become free enough to feel everything without being controlled by anything.

CHAPTER 32 — The Strength of Intuition

Intuition is not a guess. It is not anxiety dressed up as a warning. It is not imagination. It is a quiet knowledge that arrives before evidence does—the voice of your soul speaking truth before your mind can explain it.

After the crash, my intuition didn't suddenly appear. It had always been there. What changed was that I began to listen. Before, I dismissed my inner self. I called it overthinking. I argued with him. I tried to logic my way out of what I could feel in my bones. But awakening brought me back to the first language of the soul— the language of instinct, energy, and truth.

I learned that the body reacts to alignment before the mind catches up. Your chest tightens around dishonesty. Your stomach shifts around danger. Your breath changes around misalignment. The body hears what the mind tries to rationalize away.

Intuition is rarely dramatic. Fear screams, ego argues, anxiety spirals. Intuition is steady. It doesn't panic you—it clarifies you. Even when the truth is painful, intuition delivers it with calm certainty.

The more I honored my intuition, the louder and clearer it became. Trust strengthened it. Every time I listened, I taught myself: I hear you. I trust you. I am willing to follow.

And I saw how often intuition had protected me—guiding me away from what looked good but felt wrong, pulling me toward what felt right even when it scared me. It became my compass, my shield, my connection to something greater.

The strongest thing I gained wasn't a new skill. It was trust in myself. Deep, unshakable trust.

Because once you trust your intuition, life changes. Decisions become easier. Relationships become clearer. The path becomes less confusing. You stop needing constant reassurance from the outside world, because the truth is already alive inside you.

CHAPTER 33 — Integration: Becoming the Lesson

Awakening is powerful, but it isn't the end. Alignment is transformative, but it isn't enough on its own. The real shift happens when the lesson stops being something you understand and becomes something you live.

Integration is where your healing becomes behavior. Where your growth becomes consistent. Where your transformation becomes identity.

It wasn't the big moments that proved I had changed. It was the small ones. The conversation that once would've triggered me but didn't. The boundary I set without guilt. The decision I made with faith instead of fear. The moment I chose peace, even when I could've chosen reaction.

Integration tested my ego more than anything else. Because ego wants proof. It wants control. It wants to be right. It wants to win. Integration demands humility—the quiet power of letting your highest self lead.

And life began to test me, not to break me, but to anchor me. It asked: Are you still aligned when you're disappointed? Do you still trust your intuition when you're uncertain? Will you choose yourself when it's uncomfortable? Will you remain rooted when the world tries to shake you?

That's when stability arrived. Not constant happiness. Not perfection. Stability. A steadiness in my spirit. A calmness in my body. A clarity in my mind. A groundedness in my choices.

I stopped calling healing something I was "working on" and started living like the healed version of me was already here. Because she was.

Integration was the moment I realized: I am not becoming the lesson. I am the lesson.

CHAPTER 34 — Healing the Old Wounds with New Eyes

Healing doesn't end when awakening begins. Often, awakening reveals the wounds you were finally strong enough to face. Not to punish you, but to free you.

Old memories resurfaced—not as hauntings, but as invitations. I began to see patterns I had normalized. Places where I had abandoned myself. Moments where I swallowed my truth to keep peace. Times when I accepted less than I deserved and called it love, loyalty, or patience.

Pain looked different when I was no longer afraid of it. It stopped feeling like something happening to me and started feeling like information—messages from parts of me that needed attention, care, and release.

I returned to my inner child—not to relive her wounds, but to finally hold her. To become the protector she didn't have. To tell her she was safe now. To let her feel what she wasn't allowed to feel back then.

And I stopped spending my energy asking why people hurt me and started asking why I let them stay. Not as blame, but as empowerment. Because understanding my patterns gave me the power to break them.

Forgiveness became something I did for myself. Not forgetting. Not reopening doors. Not excusing harm. Forgiveness became release—closing the emotional account, reclaiming my peace, and choosing not to carry what no longer belonged to me.

The more I healed, the more I remembered myself. Healing wasn't about fixing something broken—it was about unlayering what had buried my truth. Layers of fear, conditioning, survival, and expectation fell away. And underneath them was who I had always been.

Some wounds didn't disappear completely. But they transformed into wisdom. Scars became evidence of strength. Pain became purpose.

Healing became a daily choice. A lifestyle. A commitment to never abandon my soul again.

CHAPTER 35 — Boundaries: The Protection of the Evolved Self

Alignment demanded boundaries. Not walls built from fear, but boundaries built from self-respect—structure strong enough to protect what I had worked so hard to become.

Boundaries didn't mean I loved less. They meant I loved them with clarity. They meant I stopped giving people unlimited access to my energy. They meant I stopped confusing empathy with self-sacrifice.

The truth is, access to you is earned. Proximity is earned. Influence is earned. Not everyone deserves entry into the space you've healed to create.

At first, boundaries felt uncomfortable—not because they were wrong, but because they challenged the old version of me. The version who tolerated too much. The version who explained away red flags. The version who stayed quiet to keep peace. The version who absorbed other people's emotions and called it strength.

The evolved version of me speaks clearly. Chooses consciously. Honors intuition. Protects peace. And refuses to shrink for anyone.

Boundaries revealed people's intentions. Some adjusted with grace. Some resisted. Some disappeared. Boundaries don't ruin relationships—they reveal them.

And I learned the biggest boundary wasn't with other people. It was with myself. I stopped abandoning myself to comfort others. I stopped overriding intuition with logic. I stopped staying where my spirit had already outgrown the room.

Boundaries became my protection, my medicine, my preservation. And once I learned to set them, I never returned to the life that required me to live without them.

CHAPTER 36 — The Art of Letting Go with Grace

Letting go used to feel like loss. But after awakening, I understood it differently. Letting go is not an ending—it's a clearing. A sacred release that makes room for what is meant.

Some people, patterns, and versions of myself had completed their purpose. Not because they were evil, but because they were finished. Some were chapters, not the whole book. Some were lessons, not lifetimes.

I learned to release with gratitude instead of resentment. I stopped holding endings like wounds and started honoring them like completions.

I also stopped waiting for closure from others and began giving it to myself. People don't always apologize. They don't always explain. They don't always understand what they did. But peace is not something you beg for. Peace is something you choose.

Letting go became an act of faith—faith that I was guided, protected, evolving. Faith that I wasn't losing anything meant for me. Faith that what was truly aligned would never require me to abandon myself.

And the more I released, the lighter I became. Grace made letting go beautiful, not violent. Peaceful, not chaotic. Intentional, not desperate.

Letting go wasn't losing. It was choosing.

CHAPTER 38 — Becoming a Source of Light for Others

When your spirit rises, it doesn't rise alone. It changes the atmosphere around you. Not because you try, but because you radiate.

I didn't set out to inspire anyone. I simply began living differently—more grounded, more intentional, more aware. And people felt it. They told me I made them feel calmer. Safer. Clearer. Like they could breathe.

That's when I realized: my healing wasn't meant to stay inside me.

Light is not something you force. It's something you become. A calm presence can steady chaos. A healed heart can awaken healing in others. Your story can guide people who never say they're watching.

I stepped into a quiet leadership I didn't ask for—leadership of presence. Leadership of integrity. Leadership that doesn't demand attention but naturally shifts people toward truth.

Not everyone will be ready for your light. Light exposes darkness—sometimes in others, sometimes in yourself. Some people will grow around you. Some will retreat. But your job is not too dim.

My purpose stopped being a question and became a presence. Purpose wasn't only what I did—it was how I existed. How I spoke, listened, moved, loved, discerned, and protected peace.

And my survival began to make sense. I was not saved just to continue life. I was saved to live in a way that reminded others they could rise too.

CHAPTER 39 — Divine Timing and the Unfolding of Your Path

As I lived in deeper alignment, I began to recognize a sacred rhythm beneath my life. A timing that wasn't human. A wisdom that didn't rush.

Nothing was random. Even the painful parts had a precision to them. Closed doors weren't rejection—they were redirection. Delays weren't denial—they were preparation.

What is meant for you cannot arrive too early, and it will never arrive too late. It arrives when your spirit is ready to hold it—not when your ego is impatient.

I looked back and saw protection everywhere. Times when unexpected delays saved me. Endings that freed me. Rejection that kept me from the wrong future. Silence that was instruction.

I learned something that became a rule of my life: nothing meant for your spirit will cost you your soul. Anything that requires you to shrink, abandon peace, silence intuition, or betray your truth is not aligned—no matter how good it looks on the surface.

When I stopped chasing, blessings began to follow. Not because I stopped caring, but because I stopped forcing. Surrender doesn't mean weakness. It means trust.

The path unfolds one step at a time. If you saw the whole road, you'd run ahead before you were ready. So divine timing reveals what you need, when you need it—no more, no less.

And the more I trusted timing, the more peace replaced urgency. Because I finally understood: what is meant for me cannot miss me. And what misses me was never meant.

CHAPTER 40 — Rebirth Through Alignment

This final chapter isn't an ending. It's an acknowledgement. A promise. A declaration of who I have become.

There is a moment in every journey when you pause—not because you're lost, but because you finally see it: you have become the person your past self prayed for.

Rebirth didn't happen in one instant. It happened through thousands of moments. Through decisions. Through breakdowns. Through clarity. Through surrender. Through discipline. Through choosing alignment again and again.

The crash didn't break me. It opened me up. It stripped away what didn't belong and revealed what was true. It showed me what matters, what doesn't, and who I am when everything else falls away.

Alignment became my lifestyle. Not perfection—presence. The daily practice of honoring peace, trusting intuition, protecting energy, healing intentionally, and walking forward with purpose. I stopped running from myself and started returning to myself.

My purpose is no longer a question. It is a presence. It is the way I exist. The way I love. The way I lead. The way I speak truth and hold boundaries and carry light.

I no longer live as though life is happening to me. I live as though I am co-creating with the divine. Every step is guided. Every moment is meaningful. Every shift is part of a larger design.

Gratitude became the foundation of my power—gratitude for the crash, the awakening, the lessons, the people who stayed, the people who left, and the strength that revealed itself when I didn't know it was there.

And I understand now: rebirth is not a one-time event. It is a movement. A cycle. A lifelong becoming. Every time I expand, I am reborn again. Every time I choose my truth, I align again.

I am aligned.
I am awake.
I am guided.
I am grounded.
I am evolving.
I am light.

And I will carry this life with intention for the rest of my days—because this is not the end.

This is only the start of my life.

A life-altering moment has a way of stripping everything down to what matters.

In Rebirth Through Alignment, Kiarra Schmidt traces the quiet aftermath of survival — the internal shifts that follow when life forces you to stop, listen, and begin again.

This memoir is not about the moment that changed everything, but about what came after: the slow recalibration of identity, the unraveling of old patterns, and the courage it takes to live with intention rather than instinct.

Written with honesty and restraint, Rebirth Through Alignment invites readers into the space between who we were and who we are becoming. It is a companion for those navigating healing, growth, and the quiet, often unseen work of alignment.

This is not a story about breaking.
It is a story about returning.